"A friendly introduction to a way of bein[g] [that] give your life back to you."

—Jon Kabat-Zinn, PhD, profe[ssor] University of Massachusetts Medical School and author of *Full Catastrophe Living* and *Coming to Our Senses*

"*Leaves Falling Gently* beautifully combines the wisdom of reflection, the rigor of science, and the beauty of a deeply engaged heart. Susan Bauer-Wu guides readers to live fully and gracefully with serious illness. With gentle clarity, this book offers a wealth of ideas and practices illuminating a way of being that has the power to transform our individual and collective lives."

—Shauna L. Shapiro, PhD, associate professor of counseling psychology at Santa Clara University and coauthor of *The Art and Science of Mindfulness*

"Susan Bauer-Wu describes how to live fully rather than withdrawing and feeling dread and despair when faced with a life-limiting illness. *Leaves Falling Gently* empowers readers to achieve peace of mind through mindfulness meditation and gain control over their feelings and relationships. This is a must-read for those individuals confronted with chronic, life-threatening diseases and their families."

—David S. Rosenthal, MD, professor of medicine at Harvard Medical School and past president of the American Cancer Society

"A powerful book! Susan Bauer-Wu has attacked the problems of life and death. Her book gives concrete solutions to patients and loved ones who need advice. It is an essential book for the living who may be dying. A must-read."

—Zorba Paster, MD, host of *On Your Health* on Public Radio International

"*Leaves Falling Gently* offers a direct, compelling, and practical guide to living fully even when facing serious illness. It can help us help our friends and family in the times when we so rarely know how to respond."

—Sharon Salzberg, author of *Real Happiness* and *Lovingkindness*

"Susan Bauer-Wu's book, *Leaves Falling Gently*, is the most accessible, loving and practical introduction to mindful awareness, compassion, healing and wholeness that I have ever seen. It is a precious gift for anyone who faces (or will face) life-limiting illness and death. She shows us how conditions of illness and dying, often experienced as profoundly limiting, point us to hidden wellsprings of kindness, empathy, gratitude and forgiveness beyond limits. Right through the particulars of our feelings, emotions, and reactions to illness and dying, she brings us home to the deep safety, compassion, and wholeness in the very ground of our being."

> —John Makransky, professor of Buddhism and comparative theology at Boston College

"Susan Bauer-Wu writes with the precision of a scientist, vision of a scholar, and pragmatism of someone who cares for others professionally and personally. In *Leaves Falling Gently*, she has distilled the wisdom of generations of teachers and global traditions into a practical, actionable guide for being well through the most difficult times in human life. *Leaves Falling Gently* is simple and unpretentious, yet profound. It is, quite simply, a guide to living honestly, fully, soulfully, and joyfully through even the hardest of times. What a gift! *Leaves Falling Gently* is a treasure—one to be savored and shared."

> —Ira Byock, MD, palliative care physician, professor at Dartmouth Medical School, and author of *Dying Well* and *The Four Things That Matter Most*

"This important book offers insight and inspiration for all who seek to live life fully, even in the midst of challenges beyond your control. Research, experience, and personal practice blend together to illuminate a unique approach, and Susan's writing is clearly helpful in connecting us with what matters most."

> —Ben Campbell Johnson, Ph.D.
> Professor Emeritus, Columbia Theological Seminary
> and author of *Companions in Contemplation: Reflections on the Contemplative Path.*

LEAVES

FALLING

GENTLY

—— LIVING FULLY WITH ——
SERIOUS & LIFE-LIMITING ILLNESS THROUGH
MINDFULNESS, COMPASSION
& CONNECTEDNESS

SUSAN BAUER-WU, PhD, RN

NEW HARBINGER PUBLICATIONS, INC.

Distributed in Canada by Raincoast Books

Copyright © 2011 by Susan Bauer-Wu
    New Harbinger Publications, Inc.
    5674 Shattuck Avenue
    Oakland, CA 94609
    www.newharbinger.com

Cover design by Amy Shoup; Text design by Michele Waters-Kermes;
Acquired by Catharine Meyers; Edited by Nelda Street

Library of Congress Cataloging in Publication Data on file

13   12   11

10 9 8 7 6 5 4 3 2 1   First printing

For Florence and Bill

CONTENTS

FOREWORD

Susan Bauer-Wu's wise and useful book *Leaves Falling Gently: Living Fully with Serious and Life-Limiting Illness through Mindfulness, Compassion, and Connectedness* opens three very important doors for all of us, including those who have a life-limiting illness: the door of mindfulness, the door of compassion, and the door of connectedness. In each of these areas, Dr. Bauer-Wu presents compelling scientific evidence, sensitive patient stories, and accessible reflective practices that give credence to the importance of caring for your mind, caring for your body and your heart, and caring for yourself as you travel the road of illness.

In light of this remarkable book, I feel it is important for us to remember that only 10 percent of us will die suddenly. The rest of us will face many choices about how to live with illness and how we live our dying. For many years, Dr. Bauer-Wu has been in a unique position to show us the way to the three doors of mindfulness, compassion, and connectedness. She has been a nurse who has worked in the palliative care field, she is a clinical scientist who has done foundational research on the efficacy of mindfulness practice for those going through the stem cell transplant process, and she is a long-time practitioner of meditation. Her unique background in medicine, neuroscience research, and meditation brings to the reader a great richness of experience and a true depth of wisdom, and her courage as a pathfinder is undeniable.

Also, because Dr. Bauer-Wu has firsthand knowledge of the profound benefits of mindfulness and compassion practices for those who are living with catastrophic illness, she has been able to develop specific reflective practices for those facing a life-limiting illness. Many of these practices can also serve clinicians and others who are giving care.

Dr. Bauer-Wu asks early on in her book, "What is meant by living fully?" Her response to this treasured question is that to live fully means to have a mind that is peaceful; it also means to appreciate your life and to be open to all possibilities. She suggests that living fully means being curious about life's journey, and cultivating a sense of ease, as well as meaning, even though the road may have many twists and turns. Dr. Bauer-Wu also points toward the importance of accepting all of life, even the hard parts, and when it means we must face our dying, then living that dying fully.

As the book unfolds, we learn that there are usually encounters with obstacles in this journey. Yet, we are invited to understand that these obstacles are not simply outer circumstances, but are, in fact, how we respond to our circumstances. Dr. Bauer-Wu has discovered through her research, as well as her direct work with patients, that one of the most powerful ways to work with life's challenges is through the medium of mindfulness.

As the book progresses, we learn that connected to mindfulness is the experience of compassion. We then see that compassion is a path, a practice, and a fulfillment. Dr. Bauer-Wu skillfully reminds us that it is through mindfulness that we come to the experience of compassion, and bringing mindfulness and compassion together, we open to the potential of being whole, of living our life fully, even as our life may be going through the changes of illness.

Dr. Bauer-Wu points out the interesting fact that the words "medicine" and "meditation" come from the Latin word *mederi*, meaning "to care for." This marvelous book is a manual on how we can care for ourselves, live life fully, and thereby take care of the world, as we meet illness.

Joan Halifax, PhD
Upaya Institute
Santa Fe, New Mexico

Acknowledgments

This book is the culmination of decades of learning and growing through personal, professional, and academic experiences and remarkable people who have enriched my life along the way. While it's not possible to recognize everyone whose fingerprints are on these pages, there are special individuals to whom I am especially indebted and whom I would like to gratefully acknowledge:

My parents, Florence and Bill Bauer, whose examples of love, generosity, and living with life-limiting illness provided the first seeds for this book.

The countless patients and families I have been privileged to walk alongside as they have faced the challenges of their medical conditions. I have been strengthened by our shared experiences, which inspire me to continue this meaningful work.

Those who read drafts of this book, whether sections or the entirety, and provided invaluable input and assistance: Melissa Blacker, for her clear and critical feedback with regard to language that most effectively conveys mindfulness; Angela Epshtein, for her keen and extraordinarily helpful editing suggestions; John Wu, my husband, for reading every word and sharing his sensitive insights and practical suggestions; and Rachael Whitworth, for her steady and kind presence and attention to detail.

The wonderful staff at New Harbinger, principally Angela Autry Gordon, Catharine Meyers, Jess Beebe, Kayla Sussell, and Melissa Valentine. Their guidance, input, and understanding were enormously helpful and made my first (nonacademic) book experience remarkably pleasurable.

Joan Halifax Roshi, a beloved friend and teacher. Her wise counsel, no-nonsense ways, and good humor motivate me to realize my potential and joyfully continue on the path of service.

The Upaya Institute and Zen Center "Being with Dying" faculty: Roshi Joan, Tony Back, Cynda Rushton, Gary Pasternak, Mary Taylor, and Donna Kwilosz. Our work together is nourishing and reinforces the value of contemplative practices and the power of compassionate silence.

Dan Siegel, for nudging me in just the right way, at just the right time, to get going on writing this book. His enthusiastic words opened the door within me to make it a reality.

My colleagues and students at Emory University in Atlanta, Georgia, where the collaborative spirit and stimulating learning and teaching environment continually energize me. I sincerely thank those with whom I work as part of the Nell Hodgson Woodruff School of Nursing, Emory Collaborative for Contemplative Studies, Emory-Tibet Science Initiative, and Winship Cancer Institute. A special thank-you goes to Larry Barsalou, John Dunne, and Stephanie Grossman for their valued friendship.

Jon Kabat-Zinn, Saki Santorelli, Melissa Blacker, and Florence Meleo-Meyer, for their vision and tireless efforts to establish and develop the University of Massachusetts Center for Mindfulness in Medicine, Health Care, and Society, and for their support and mentoring to me.

Treasured friends and colleagues who have helped to sustain me, undimmed by distance or circumstances: Katherine Brown-Saltzman and Janice Post-White for our biennial girls' spa getaways (formerly "writing retreats") and dancing with the dolphins in Hawaii; Mary Cooley for being such a dear and impeccable collaborator; Adam Engle for sticking by me on the trail (even at eighteen thousand feet); Lynn Kutler for her kind heart and for caring deeply about spreading mindfulness; Rolf Ludwig for our heartwarming conversations over German beer and for tenderly calling me "Bauerle"; Arti Prasad for her thoughtfulness and dedication to promoting integrative medicine; Elana Rosenbaum for her joie de vivre in all we've embarked on together over the last twelve years (Retreats to Renew, Hope Lodge group, research with bone-marrow transplant patients, and so on); Celia Schiffer, Ellen Lavoie Smith, Suzanne Hanser, and Amy Sullivan,

✖

each for their steadfast friendship; Tenzin Sonam, my Tibetan brother, for his sincerity and for doing cartwheels with me on the ridge; Sharon Tucker for her trustworthy advice during our many long phone conversations; and Jan Zeller for being a superb mentor and, now, dear friend.

My wonderful family, who have loved and supported me throughout all of the different chapters of my life: my siblings Margie, Billy, Robin, and John; my sister-in-law Lori; my brothers-in-law Chris and Bob; my cousins, especially Cathy and Linda; and my terrific nephews Chris, Sean, Matt, Jason, Jordan, Dan, Tom, and Nick; sweet and graceful Aunt Elinore; steady and strong Uncle Butch; my endearing Uncle Howard, for his cheerful phone calls filled with Brooklyn wisdom; and my delightful stepdaughters, Marissa and Adrienne, whom I enjoy tremendously and who often bring a smile to my face and make me proud.

And finally, my partner and best friend, John, whose unwavering love, kindheartedness, brilliance, and generous spirit shine brightly and help me to clearly see what matters most.

INTRODUCTION

Enough. These few words are enough.
If not these words, this breath.
If not this breath, this sitting here.
This opening to the life
we have refused
again and again
until now.
Until now.

—David Whyte

Gary, a successful businessman with a self-described type A personality, was fifty-eight years old when he learned that the cancer he'd had for many years had progressed and the available treatment options offered little hope of achieving long-term remission. He knew that his time was indeed limited. His mind raced with worries about how long he had left, whether he would be able to complete projects, what would happen to his family and his business, how his body would feel as the disease progressed, and how he would die. He grew frustrated by his increasing physical limitations. Anger, irritation, sadness, and anxiety infused his waking moments, and he felt disconnected from the world around him and those he loved most. Recognizing that this was not how he wanted to live his remaining precious months or years, he searched to find ways that he could gain peace of mind, meaning, and a sense of control amid all of the unease and uncertainty. With encouragement from his wife, Christine, and his health care team, Gary participated in a program that taught mindfulness and compassion-meditation practices. Several weeks later, he shared his perspective: "The program has changed the whole quality of my life, and the meditation practices have become a daily ritual. It has been one of the most important parts of my healing. It lowered my anxiety and increased my sense of control. When I meditate, I feel relaxed and refreshed. The more I practice, the calmer I become. Before, I was always someone who fretted about things. Now I'm focused on the pleasure of the moment, and the days are not agonizing—even if I'm feeling really ill."

Leaves Falling Gently is for anyone with a life-limiting illness who genuinely wants to live as fully as possible. *Life-limiting illness* refers to serious and progressive medical conditions that limit the quality *and* length of life. With practical and easy-to-follow exercises, this book will enrich your final years, months, and days with its wisdom. It offers greater peace of mind, comfort, and connection with others and with what gives life meaning. Specifically, we will explore the use of mindfulness and compassion practices, including personal reflection and guided meditations, to cultivate a clear and equanimous mind; vividness in daily experiences; and the interpersonal qualities of gratitude, generosity, forgiveness, and love. The goal of this book is to help you to feel whole and live well, despite changes and challenges beyond your control, and ultimately to die with serenity.

The Author's Perspective

The impetus for this book is my combined professional experience as a registered nurse in oncology and palliative care, a trained teacher in mindfulness-based stress reduction, and a mind-body researcher with a particular interest in the clinical applications of meditation during serious illness and at the end of life. I also bring my personal experience as someone who has practiced mindfulness and compassion meditation for many years, and who has walked the path of devastating illness and death with family members and close friends. Time and time again, I have witnessed the benefits of mindfulness and compassion practices and listened to the voices of those who have been positively transformed. The meditations and other reflective practices described in this book have been specifically adapted for people facing the unique physical, mental, and spiritual challenges of life-limiting illness and have been used successfully in clinical and research settings by me, my colleagues, and others.

Living with Life-Limiting Illness

Coming face to face with what is generally considered to be an incurable illness can be overwhelming in every sense of the word. Physically, everyday activities may require more energy. And despite your best efforts, you may not be able to do what you used to do, or you may even need help from others. You may experience discomforts like pain, nausea, or extreme fatigue. Mentally, you may struggle with feeling unwell and also with coming to terms with the knowledge that you likely will not overcome and be cured of the illness. Your mind may be filled with fear of the unknown and the future, or with regret for things you have or haven't done. You may feel so anxious about running out of time that the anxiety is paralyzing. You may also feel saddened or depressed by all of the changes and losses before you. Spiritually, you may try to make sense of or question what is happening to you. You may be drawn to explore the meaning of your life and to wonder about your death. Socially, you may notice that your relationships with loved ones and friends are shifting, perhaps becoming more distant or becoming closer. You may realize that you need to figure out new ways to have fun together, be intimate, and have difficult conversations.

Living Fully Is Possible

What is meant by *living fully*? While the specific answer is different for everyone, I'd like to offer one definition that I will use to guide this book.

3

"Living fully" means to live with a sense of ease, contentment, curiosity, and meaning. It means accepting all that life has to offer, both its pleasures and its stings, and being open to the infinite possibilities of experience as each day unfolds. It means saying yes to what *is* possible despite frailty, disability, or even impending death. Feeling overwhelmed is understandable, although it is optional. Nevertheless, living fully *is* possible.

Obstacles to Living Fully

Common mental and emotional obstacles impede your ability to live fully. For example, you could feel frozen by the fear of getting sicker and the fear of dying, or feel consumed by the disease and its treatment. You might also angrily resist changes that are beyond your control, put up walls between you and those you care about most, withdraw from the world, dwell in the past, judge your own and others' actions and abilities as inadequate, and focus on what's wrong with you and your situation. These obstacles are actually internal: they are mental constructions and emotional reactions that make a difficult situation worse. They also hold you back and cloud the precious moments that you are alive.

Overcoming Mental and Emotional Obstacles

Learning how to live fully by overcoming mental and emotional obstacles through the cultivation of mindfulness, compassion, and a sense of connectedness is at the heart of this book.

Mindfulness

Mindfulness involves intentionally paying attention to the present moment with a spirit of curiosity and openness. It is a way of being that includes awareness of whatever you're experiencing—through your five senses, your internal bodily sensations, your thoughts and emotions—while having an attitude of receptivity and gentleness. It is simply noticing things as they are, without adding stories, judging experiences as good or bad, clinging to what you like or fear losing, or resisting what you don't like.

You can cultivate this quality of mindfulness through formal practices, such as intentionally being aware of breathing and tuning in to bodily sensations, and informally through awareness of everyday activities like brushing your teeth, eating, walking, or washing the dishes. As mindfulness develops, positive mental and emotional qualities emerge. You see things more clearly. Just as yoga makes you more physically flexible, mindfulness practices make you more mentally flexible and better able to "go with the flow." When you are mindful, you have emotional balance, with fewer extreme highs and lows, and a sense of spaciousness and inquisitiveness toward whatever arises. You can catch yourself when your mind is caught in a downward spiral of negative thinking or when other mental obstacles trip you up. Rather than react automatically, you respond more thoughtfully and are more likely to accept whatever is happening.

Mindfulness meditation and other approaches that cultivate mindfulness have been around for millennia. However, the integration into conventional Western medical settings began over thirty years ago, with the establishment of the mindfulness-based stress reduction (MBSR) program by Jon Kabat-Zinn and his colleagues at the University of Massachusetts Medical School in Worcester. Research evidence is mounting (Bohlmeijer et al. 2010; Grossman et al. 2004; Ledesma and Kumano 2009), and as such, MBSR programs are now available in hundreds of clinical settings, on every continent except Antarctica. The mindfulness practices described in this book are rooted in MBSR, yet have been expanded and modified specifically for people who are living with serious illness.

Compassion

Compassion involves opening up your heart. It is the genuine desire to alleviate mental and physical suffering—for yourself and others. As compassion grows, it fosters kindness, joy, and receptivity. It softens the shield around your heart. You can cultivate compassion through personal reflection, "heart" and forgiveness meditations, and acts of kindness and altruism. Recent research has demonstrated the benefits of cultivating compassion and kindness in improving health and well-being (Pace et al. 2009; Fredrickson et al. 2008). In my work with people who are very sick, I have observed the enormous power of these approaches to tap into a person's heart and generate feelings of love, gratitude, happiness in others' good fortune, generosity, and forgiveness. One person, named Mary, comes to mind. She found that, in time and with practice, she was able to soften the hard shell around her heart and forgive and be grateful to her loved ones. This was a tremendous relief to Mary, and she was then better able to enjoy her life and feel more connected with her family and friends.

Connectedness

Together, mindfulness and compassion naturally provide fertile ground for a sense of connectedness to flourish, connectedness with what gives life meaning: with family and friends, with simple pleasures and personal priorities, with nature, and with the world in general. Collectively and synergistically, awareness (mindfulness), openheartedness (compassion), and interconnectedness help us to feel whole.

Healing and Feeling Whole

Feeling whole corresponds with healing. In fact, the words "whole" and "heal" originate from the same word. *Healing* can be defined as restoring a person's sense of wholeness and integrity. So while you perhaps cannot be cured in the traditional biomedical sense (for example, getting rid of evidence of the disease), it is certainly possible for you to heal and feel whole, even when your physical body doesn't work the way it used to or when your days are limited. When you feel whole, your experiences and relationships are richer, more vibrant, and more meaningful. In essence, you live fully.

How to Use This Book

This book is organized into three parts: "Mindfulness," "Compassion," and "Connectedness." Within each part are chapters that explore specific topics, including both information and guided experiential practices. Every chapter brings to light the issues people living with life-limiting illness face and includes simple and practical exercises. I'll share accounts of actual people to illustrate how others going through a similar experience have learned and grown from doing the practices. I will also describe information on clinical and neuroscience research to explain how these contemplative approaches work and could help you.

I recommend that you read and experience one part of the book at a time, because each part is built on the previous one. For example, begin with part 1, "Mindfulness." A foundation in mindfulness is essential for compassion to develop ("Compassion" is part 2). Together, mindfulness plus compassion allows for "Connectedness" (part 3) to blossom. I recommend that you go through the book sequentially once, and then go back and skip around to sections that you're interested in revisiting.

A Secular Practice, Not a Religious One

Of note is that the principles and guided exercises in this book are secular and do not ascribe to any particular religion. While mindfulness, compassion, and connectedness are fundamental to Buddhist philosophy, this is not a book about Buddhism or any religion per se. Anyone can appreciate and benefit from cultivating these basic human qualities, which are shared across many religions and cultures.

Similarly, the term *meditation* in this book can be interpreted more generally as "reflective practice" rather than a particular technique. It is interesting to consider that the words "meditation" and "medicine" come from the same root, the Latin word *mederi*, which means "to care for." So you can consider the meditation practices to be a way for you to care for yourself with kindness and gentleness.

Experiencing and Practicing Are Essential

Every chapter includes essential experiential practices consisting of meditations and reflective writing. For these practices, I suggest that you *read, pause, do,* and *reflect.*

Read	Read each phrase.
Pause	Take a moment to absorb the words.
Do	Experience what the words convey, and then move on to the next phrase or bullet.
Reflect	Consider what new insights you may have gained from the practice.

Simply reading the meditation and writing practices will not suffice. In order for you to benefit, you must experience and practice them. That's why they're called *practices.* The more you practice, the more you will tap into and fine-tune the qualities. Then they will eventually become a natural extension of who you are. Research supports this direct association between practice and benefit (Carmody and Baer 2008). Doing the practices will translate into your *being* more mindful and compassionate and, in turn, more connected, which will help you to feel more whole and live more fully.

PART 1

~

MINDFULNESS

1

~

WHAT IS MINDFULNESS?

The quality of our experience, moment by moment, will determine the quality of our lives.

—Matthieu Ricard

Mindfulness is our capacity to intentionally bring awareness to present-moment experience with an attitude of openness and curiosity. It is being awake to the fullness of our lives right now, through engaging the five senses and noticing the changing landscapes of our minds without holding on to or pushing away any of it.

Mindfulness is a way of being and relating to ourselves, our circumstances, one another, and the world around us. It's actually an innate human quality. Consider how a child attends to licking an ice cream cone or stroking a puppy. The child is naturally fully immersed in the experience of tasting and sensing the sweet, cool ice cream on her tongue, or touching the soft fur and looking into the eyes of the puppy. The child isn't deliberately trying to be mindful; she just is. However, as we get older, we generally lose touch with such freshness and curiosity as life experiences condition our minds and fill them with expectations, facts, rules, plans, worries, regrets, and fantasies. The busyness of our modern high-tech and low-touch society also takes us away from fully experiencing our day-to-day lives. Mindfulness is remembering who we are and befriending our experiences, whether pleasant or unpleasant. It is about coming home to ourselves and to the truth of our lives in this moment with openness, kindness, and acceptance.

When you are living with a serious medical condition, it's easy to get carried away with asking yourself questions like *Why?* and *What if?* and get caught up in the storm of your mind. Mindfulness can help you to ground yourself to what is happening right now, then thoughtfully respond and make decisions that are consistent with your values and needs. The truth is that the present moment is what you know for sure, and you can play an active role in how you live right now. Mindfulness gives you a sense of being in charge at a time when circumstances seem beyond your control.

You can cultivate mindfulness through the relatively simple practices explored throughout this book.

Experiencing Things as They Are

Mindfulness involves opening up to whatever is happening—in your body, your mind, and your environment—and experiencing things as they are without being compelled to change anything. It doesn't mean that you will always like what you are experiencing. It's normal to have moments when you feel confused, frustrated, and agitated. When you can allow yourself to ease into this moment and just notice rather than shut off, resist, or react, you will see that there is an ebb and flow to the experience and that things don't stay static. Just being with and noticing whatever is occurring can help you to learn much about yourself and your relationship with the world around you. In turn, a sense of spaciousness and acceptance naturally emerges.

Responding vs. Reacting

Life is full of concerns, disappointments, and annoyances: receiving the bad news that your disease has progressed or your spouse has lost his job, waiting for overdue communication from someone you care about, getting yelled at, being with someone who continually presses your buttons (and doesn't stop when asked), or being put on hold for a long time, only to find that a computer voice eventually "helps" you. Some variation on these examples likely comes up every day, challenging you and threatening your sense of serenity, security, and integrity. The question is: what do you do in such circumstances?

Reacting is automatic, like a knee-jerk reflex. You aren't even aware of how you're reacting until sometime later, or maybe you never even realize what you've done. Reactions are usually a combination of thoughts (like *I don't deserve this*), emotions (like dejection or anger), actions (like yelling, turning away, or shutting down), and physical experiences in the body (like muscles tensing). Some extreme, and unfortunately fairly common, aggressive reactions include lashing out with strong and hurtful words, slamming doors, throwing things or physically harming someone, or abruptly hanging up the phone. Other more-passive reactions include disengaging from others by shutting down, being cold or rude, walking out, or running away. Regardless of the specific behavior, reacting often has detrimental consequences. You will likely feel worse as a result. You may be self-deprecating and harbor regret for what you've done. You may harden your heart and put up walls. Usually your words and actions negatively affect you and others when you react, and sometimes relationships become irreparably damaged. The bottom line is that reacting can lead to significant consequences that diminish your sense of well-being and interfere with your ability to live fully.

A more helpful approach would be to respond rather than react. Mindfulness plays a critical role here. *Responding* means being fully cognizant of the situation and conscious of what you're doing in response to something that is threatening or challenging. Being mindful helps you to be in control and catch yourself before you react. When you're mindful, you can deliberately pause and momentarily step back to assess what's happening. With spacious awareness, you become a curious observer of your experience. You are vividly aware of your experience, yet you aren't lost in it. With calm understanding, you can objectively consider the different potential outcomes. From this place of clarity, groundedness, and strength, you can thoughtfully speak, take action, or choose to do nothing. When you respond rather than react, you make better decisions and are less likely to suffer from negative repercussions. Ultimately, you feel happier and more whole, and your relationships are stronger.

Catching Yourself on Autopilot

Have you ever found yourself driving with no recollection of what you drove past during the preceding minutes? Have you ever finished a meal and realized that you didn't remember tasting any of the food? Have you ever taken a shower without noticing the water and soap on your skin? Chances are you've had at least one of these *automatic pilot* experiences. This is looking without seeing and hearing without listening. Essentially you are doing without *experiencing*, because your mind is somewhere else. Mindfulness is that instant when you catch yourself on autopilot. When you catch yourself in this manner, simply smile and gently return to the experience.

How to Approach Mindfulness Practice

In his seminal book *Full Catastrophe Living: Using the Wisdom of Your Body and Mind to Face Stress, Pain, and Illness* (1990), Jon Kabat-Zinn describes seven qualities of mind that are foundational for mindfulness-meditation practice: nonjudging, patience, beginner's mind, trust, nonstriving, acceptance, and letting go. *Nonjudging* means neutrally observing what is happening within and around you, without being quick to make value judgments, such as good or bad, right or wrong. *Patience* means allowing learning and growing through meditation practice to unfold over time, without rushing or forcing the process. *Beginner's mind* means having a fresh and inquisitive perspective as if you were experiencing a situation for the first time. *Trust* refers to believing in yourself and trusting your intuition, recognizing that you are the authority who knows your body and your feelings. *Nonstriving* means not being driven to attain a particular goal. In meditation, you're not trying to feel a certain way, do anything special, or get anything specific out of it. *Acceptance* means taking things as they are in the present, with whatever is occurring or however you feel. This doesn't mean you have to like the situation, but accepting is essential to healing and positive self-change. Last, *letting go* involves not clinging to or resisting particular thoughts or emotions. You can watch them come and go, without letting them take hold and consume you.

How you approach mindfulness practice matters. Throughout this book, we will keep returning to these qualities, which are essential for the cultivation of mindfulness and through which your life will be enriched in meaningful ways.

What Mindfulness Is Not

To understand what mindfulness is, it may be helpful to clarify what mindfulness is not. Mindfulness is *not*:

- Trying to achieve a special state of mind. Mindfulness allows mind states to naturally surface and be noticed, but it doesn't force them to change.

- Going into a trance. Rather, mindfulness is being alert and attentive to what is happening.

- Thinking positive thoughts. Positive, negative, and neutral thoughts may all come to mind and are regarded equally.

- Distracting yourself or imagining you are somewhere else. Mindfulness is the antithesis of distraction and imagery. Rather than take your mind off or away from actual circumstances, mindfulness involves attending to what is happening in the present moment, even if it's unpleasant.

- "Doing" anything. In its simplest and purest sense, mindfulness is a way of being and is not about doing anything.

- Religious. The essence of mindfulness is accessible to everyone regardless of faith tradition.

- Complicated or far out. On the contrary, mindfulness is return-ing to a very simple way of being and relating to yourself, others, and your circumstances.

- Exclusively Eastern. While mindfulness is a foundation of Asian cultures and religions, especially Buddhism, there is nothing particularly exotic or Eastern about living attentively and with kindness. The principles of mindfulness are universal.

What's the Evidence?

Research on mindfulness has burgeoned over the last decade, with the first studies published nearly thirty years ago. Emerging studies are beginning to elucidate the underlying mechanisms of mindfulness (such as what happens in the brain and other parts of the body when you are mindful) and the effects of mindfulness meditation and related practices on health and well-being.

Changes in the Brain

You can learn mindfulness through practices like mindfulness medita-tion, which is considered a type of mental training. Numerous studies have shown that people without prior experience in mindfulness meditation can, in fact, transform the way their brains work and enhance their cognitive, emotional, and physiological functioning as a result of mindfulness training (Brefczynski-Lewis et al. 2007; Davidson et al. 2003; Chiesa and Serretti 2010; Slagter et al. 2007). At a very basic level, we are able to acquire mind-fulness skills because of *neuroplasticity*, which literally means that cells in the brain, called *neurons*, are plastic, or malleable. Essentially, the brain has the ability to alter its structure and function depending on the parts of the brain that are used. When regions of the brain are activated over and over again, those connections get strengthened. Conversely, when areas of the brain are used infrequently, they become weakened. Consider the analogy of exercising: The more you exercise, the stronger your muscles become. When you don't exercise, your muscles atrophy. Mindfulness meditation, like other kinds of mental training, strengthens areas of the brain that are used during the practice, while other areas become weaker as a result of not being used. Regions of the brain that are associated with mindfulness include those areas involved in focusing attention, adapting to unexpected changes, monitoring and perceiving your environment, and perceiving internal body sensations (Jha, Krompinger, and Baime 2007; Slagter et al. 2007; Moore and Malinowski 2009; Lutz, Slagter, et al. 2008; Farb et al. 2007). Mindfulness has been shown to decrease activation of the *amygdala*, which is the area of the brain associated with fear and stress perception (Brefczynski-Lewis et al. 2007), and lessen ruminations and distractive thinking (Jain et al. 2007). Neuroscience research points to how mindfulness training can help you to be less fearful and stressed out, more focused, better able to go with the flow, and more aware of what is happening around you and consequently to respond wisely and be in tune with your body and its needs.

Quality of Life and Symptoms

Clinical studies have demonstrated the benefits of mindfulness training in people with serious chronic health conditions, such as cancer (Bauer-Wu et al. 2008; Carlson et al. 2007), HIV or AIDS (Creswell et al. 2009), multiple sclerosis (Grossman et al. 2010), solid-organ transplant (Kreitzer et al. 2005), and heart failure (Sullivan et al. 2009). While many of the studies are limited in scope or methods and more research is needed, the collective findings are consistent and suggest positive effects on quality of life, psychological well-being, and symptoms such as pain, sleep disturbances, and fatigue. For example, in my research with cancer patients hospitalized for autologous bone marrow/stem cell transplant, we have consistently found significant reduction in pain and anxiety, and greater sense of happiness, after thirty-minute mindfulness training sessions (Bauer-Wu et al. 2008). We also found decreased heart and breathing rates, which are markers for less stress reactivity in the body. Paul Grossman, a clinical researcher in

Europe, led a well-designed study of relapsed multiple sclerosis patients and found that an eight-week mindfulness training program enhanced health-related quality of life and alleviated symptoms of depression and fatigue (Grossman et al. 2010). In other research, Mary Jo Kreitzer, Cynthia Gross, and colleagues at the University of Minnesota found that patients who had gone through a solid-organ transplant and were suffering from sleep disturbances reported improvements in their sleep patterns after they participated in a mindfulness-based stress reduction (MBSR) program (Kreitzer et al. 2005).

Effects on the Body

Besides improving the way people feel, mindfulness training has been shown to lead to positive changes in biological outcomes. Because mindfulness training promotes changes in the brain that foster emotional balance (less-extreme highs and lows) and help us to see more clearly and not perceive circumstances to be so threatening, it can initiate a complex cascade of chemical processes in the body. Chemical processes in the brain subsequently affect all body organs as well as the immune system, which plays a key role in fighting infections and controlling many diseases, like cancer, HIV, and AIDS. Also, the cascade of chemical processes influences inflammation, which is associated with the development and exacerbation of serious health conditions, such as heart disease, cancer, rheumatoid arthritis, and neurological conditions. Mindfulness training has been shown to enhance immune function in people with cancer (Carlson et al. 2007; Witek-Janusek et al. 2008) and HIV or AIDS (Creswell et al. 2009; Jam et al. 2010) and to lower a key inflammatory marker called C-reactive protein, which is linked to heart disease and diabetes (Dalen et al. 2010).

Mental Health

Mindfulness training has also been shown to be very effective for people with mental health conditions, like recurrent clinical depression (Teasdale et al. 2002), anxiety and panic disorders (Goldin, Ramel, and Gross 2009;

Kim et al. 2010), and substance abuse (Witkiewitz and Bowen 2010). John Teasdale and Zindel Segal, along with their colleagues, have demonstrated that people at risk for recurrent depression benefit from a mindfulness-based program called *mindfulness-based cognitive therapy* (MBCT), which specifically lessens the chances of severe depression to recur (Teasdale et al. 2002). MBCT is modeled after the popular *mindfulness-based stress reduction* (MBSR) program that was established at the University of Massachusetts Medical School over thirty years ago. Both are group programs conducted weekly over a period of eight weeks and include home meditation practice (recommended formal practice of forty-five minutes daily, six days per week). To date, much of the research on mindfulness practices for people with health problems has been based on MBSR, MBCT, or modified versions of those programs.

Benefits of Practice

While you may immediately feel better (such as more comfortable and relaxed) after just a brief guided meditation, research consistently shows that the amount of mindfulness training a person is engaged in is directly associated with the magnitude of effects (Carmody and Baer 2008; Lazar et al. 2005). The amount of self-directed practice (with or without listening to guided meditation recordings) and the frequency of meetings with a trained mindfulness instructor (individually or in a group setting) predict how much a person will get out of the training. Essentially, the more you do the mindfulness practices, the greater the benefits. Practicing regularly (for example, several days a week) is clearly superior to doing it once in a while. It's like flossing your teeth; daily flossing will keep your gums healthier than if you floss only periodically.

Are You Ready?

Neuroscience research shows us that the old adage "You can't teach an old dog new tricks" no longer applies. I've heard countless people say that they can't be mindful because they are driven to distraction and can't stop or sit still. The research data and my own experience indicate otherwise. However, as behavior-change theories underscore, adopting a new behavior or stopping an old one necessitates *readiness*, which is a genuine desire and intention to learn or change a behavior (Prochaska and Velicer 1997). As you embark on the journey of cultivating mindfulness, remember that your intention, your commitment and self-discipline to practice, and how you approach your practice will have a substantial effect on what transpires.

Cultivating Mindfulness

The meditation practices described throughout this book are intended to help you cultivate mindfulness in such a way that it becomes integrated with who you are. The practices are not intended to be something special that you do only at particular times or when you feel a particular way. Rather, I hope that you will be mindful throughout each day, and that mindfulness will help you ride the waves of ups and downs with equanimity, clarity, and fullness.

Regular Practice

It is essential to engage in a regular mindfulness meditation practice in order to cultivate mindfulness and have it permeate your everyday life. As described previously, studies consistently show that practicing makes a difference and directly relates to how much benefit you gain. You may feel better after you meditate for a half hour, but the effects won't be sustained if you do it only once in a while.

Neutral Point of Focus

The first step in developing mindfulness is learning to stabilize the mind. Our minds have a tendency to keep busy during our waking hours (and for some of us, even when we are sleeping!). The mind naturally bounces from one idea to another. Paying attention to a neutral point of focus is the easiest way to stabilize the mind and get you centered, kind of like how an anchor stops a boat from drifting aimlessly or getting tossed around in a storm. At a moment's notice, you can return to the experience of the present moment simply by bringing awareness to an easily accessible, neutral point of focus. *Neutral* in this regard means that it doesn't evoke a strong emotion or physical reaction; it doesn't upset or excite you, and you generally feel indifferent toward it.

The Breath

The breath is a common neutral point of focus, because it is always with us. As long as we are alive, we are breathing. For most people, breathing is not effortful. It is just there with us every moment we are alive. We don't try to breathe; it just happens incessantly, much like how the waves of the ocean continue to meet the shore.

If Breathing Is Challenging

However, for some people, breathing poses considerable challenges due to underlying health problems. If that is the case for you, then the breath would not be a neutral focus. In some instances, bringing attention to the sensations of breathing could cause more discomfort. If you have trouble breathing, then it's important to identify another neutral point of focus that you could use as an anchor to help you return to the present moment time and time again. This anchor ought to be a body part or specific bodily experience rather than something external to you, because you need to be able to use that point of focus as a resource regardless of where you are; it must be with you at all times. Some possible alternatives include a hand, forearm, foot, or earlobe. You will need to explore and identify what part of your body is neutral for you.

~ MEDITATION PRACTICE ~
Awareness of Breathing

- Settle into a comfortable position, which may be sitting, lying down, or standing.

- Bring awareness to sensations associated with the air entering your body. This may be at the nostrils, the mouth, or both. You may notice the air temperature (such as coolness) and quality (such as moist or dry) as it enters your body.

- Notice the air as it moves down into your body, filling your lungs and expanding your belly.

- Be aware of the brief pause between the inbreath and the outbreath.

- Then, as you exhale, notice your belly falling and the air moving from your abdomen through your chest and neck, and out through your nostrils or mouth.

- Do this for a few cycles of breathing in and breathing out, being aware of the sensations of the air coming into and filling your body and then being released and leaving your body.

- To help you settle and focus, especially in the beginning as you explore this practice, you may choose to say to yourself: *Breathing in, I know I am breathing in. Breathing out, I know I am breathing out.*

- Don't try to change your breathing; just allow yourself to breathe in a natural and comfortable way. Simply bring awareness to the experience, riding the waves of inbreath and outbreath.

~ MEDITATION PRACTICE ~

Alternative (If Breathing Is Challenging)

- Settle into a comfortable position, which may be sitting, lying down, or standing.

- Mentally scan your body and identify a neutral part of it. This is a part of your body that doesn't trigger strong emotions, memories, or discomfort. Some examples of potentially neutral body parts are hands, forearms, lips, earlobes, and feet. You know best what areas feel neutral to you. Choose to focus on a single body part on one side of your body.

- Bring awareness to that body part. Notice internal sensations associated with it, such as tingling or pulsing. Notice any external sensations, like cool air or the feeling of clothes or linens.

- For a few minutes, imagine yourself breathing in and breathing out from this area of your body.

Each Day...

During the day, if you find that your mind is racing, you are having trouble focusing, or you're feeling overwhelmed with anger, frustration, or despair, just *STOP*:

S   *Stop* what you are doing, and pause for a moment.

T   *Take* a breath mindfully, and be aware of the experience of the air coming into your body and filling it, then being released.

If you have trouble breathing, $T = $ *Tune in* to a neutral part of your body and imagine yourself breathing into and out of that area.

O   *Observe* your thoughts and feelings. Just notice them in an inquisitive and dispassionate way, without getting caught up in them.

P   *Proceed* with whatever you were doing, with awareness and gentleness.

Keep in Mind

Mindfulness is a way of being and remembering who you are and befriending your experiences, whether pleasant or unpleasant. You can return to the breath or another neutral point of focus anytime and anyplace—whenever you feel agitated, confused, or overwhelmed—to re-center and feel more grounded. As you embark on the journey of cultivating mindfulness, remember that your intention, your commitment and self-discipline, and your approach toward the practice will have a considerable effect on how you will feel and what will emerge.

2

TUNING IN TO YOUR BODY

So before we convince ourselves that our bodies are too this or too that, shouldn't we get more in touch with how wonderful it is to have a body in the first place, no matter what it looks or feels like?

—Jon Kabat-Zinn, *Full Catastrophe Living*

The idea of *tuning in*—to look, listen, and engage with your body in an intimate dialogue about what you are actually feeling in a particular moment—is foreign and even a turnoff to many people, especially to those who have a serious physical illness. You may wonder why in the world you would want to be more aware of your body at a time when your body is failing and you're not feeling well.

Tuning in is an entry into accepting your body as it is right now, which allows for a larger sense of acceptance. Tuning in helps you to realize that unpleasant physical symptoms, like pain or nausea, are not always the same; they actually change from moment to moment. It allows you to be aware of important body cues and to choose how to respond to those cues. By tuning in, you may recognize that what you're feeling may not be significantly different from how you felt hours, days, or even weeks before, so you may be less likely to panic when you feel discomfort. Tuning in is an opening for you to be aware of your tendencies to automatically react and create meaning about what you feel in your body. It is also an opportunity for you to be conscious of what is right or healthy in your body. You come to realize that all of you is *not* broken, and that you are much, much more than a diagnosis or a body with a disease.

Befriending Your Body

You, like many people with a life-limiting illness, may feel that your body has betrayed you. You may feel frustrated that the years of trying to take good care of yourself have not prevented devastating illness from rearing its ugly head. Why would you ever want to be friends with your body, a body that has let you down?

Befriending your body doesn't mean that you have to like what is happening to it. Rather, it means that you are kind and gentle toward your body and that you sincerely listen to it as you would your best friend. You are open to joining, being with, and accepting your body with all its frailties and imperfections. This allows you to come to a place of deep inner knowing and acceptance, which fosters healing on many levels.

Consider for a moment these questions: Does harboring anger about feeling betrayed by your body serve you in any way? What if you (metaphorically) joined hands and made friends with your body?

Awareness of Sensations as Just Sensations

A first step toward tuning in to your body is being aware of sensations as just sensations. This involves becoming a curious and detached observer. More often than not, the tendency is for the mind to have a single, labeled concept of what is happening in the body, like "pain," or to interpret what it means. For example, new pain means that the disease has progressed. However, if you step back and curiously observe what your body is feeling, you realize that pain is not just one big overwhelming "thing," but rather a constellation of many subtle bodily sensations, such as dullness, sharpness, aching, or throbbing, that likely change from moment to moment. You may also notice breaks in the sensations and moments of not feeling anything. Seeing sensations as mere sensations, and noticing their nuanced qualities and fluctuations, gives them less power over you.

The Story around the Sensations

More often than not, it is human nature to conjure up a story or narrative around what is happening in your body or your life. The stories are not grounded in fact or what you know for sure in the present moment; rather they are nightmares of what might be, future-oriented fantasies, judgments, regrets, or instances of clinging to what occurred in the past. An example from everyday life is being unable to find your wallet and immediately panicking and conjuring up a story about its having been stolen. Stories are automatic and can carry you away. They agitate the mind, which in turn agitates the body and shakes up your world in general.

For someone who has a serious illness, the mental stories and judgments can easily jump to worst-case scenario or to self-blame. The stories can take you through a horrific adventure in your mind, to the point where your body responds as if it were actually experiencing the story. For example, a new discomfort can send you into a state of panic, accompanied by a rapidly beating heart, shallow breathing, indigestion, and difficulty sleeping, if you imagine it to mean that your disease is worsening or you did something to cause it. Your thoughts, or the story, can consume you and repeat over and over in your mind, overshadowing everything else that is actually happening in your life to the point where you don't even notice any goodness around you.

The terms "pain" and "suffering" are often used interchangeably, but there is a significant distinction between the two. *Pain* is an unpleasant physical signal that tells you something is not right in your body. *Suffering* is how you relate to it; it is the meaning or interpretation (or the story) your mind creates in response to the physical signal. The meaning you construct about the pain and how you interpret it actually determine your experience, which can indeed magnify the unpleasantness. This is illustrated in the ancient parable about an arrow. The arrow, by chance, enters your arm and causes pain. Then you respond by taking the arrow shaft and driving it in farther. The arrow entering the arm was inevitable. However, driving the arrow deeper was optional; doing so made the experience exponentially worse. In this example, driving in the arrow represents the mental story called *I deserve to be in pain, This is just the beginning; more pain will come my way*, or *Something awful is happening*. Such stories are truly angst filled, and each version leads to more unnecessary suffering. It's amazing how our minds take an unpleasant sensation and make up a complicated story that creates or perpetuates fears and worries. Mindfulness practices, as described in this book, can help you catch yourself when your mind goes off in the story.

A woman with cancer with whom I worked shared this comment after learning and practicing mindfulness:

> *I have found that sometimes when I feel a little twinge and start to get worried, I catch myself. I turn my attention to what I am feeling and imagine breathing into that area, and then I can sense it easing. This keeps me from getting panicky or scared.*

Unpleasant Symptoms

Unpleasant physical symptoms are almost universally part of having a life-limiting illness. The particular symptoms you experience and the degree of discomfort you have depend on the specific disease and treatment, and are influenced by your age, genetics, and past experiences. Common unpleasant symptoms include fatigue, pain, nausea, numbness, weakness, and itching.

It is important to note the differences between acute and chronic symptoms. *Acute symptoms* are physical sensations that come on quickly or increase sharply in intensity but last for only a limited time. They can be very severe, like a rating of 9 or 10 on a scale of 0 to 10 (with 0 being no discomfort and 10 being the most discomfort you could imagine ever experiencing). Acute symptoms are to be neither tolerated nor ignored. Severe pain and other symptoms are valuable messengers of important information about the body. It's critical that you listen to your body and respond wisely.

Chronic symptoms are unpleasant sensations and bodily experiences that linger for weeks, months, or years. They fluctuate in intensity and are generally tolerable. These are the symptoms that you are told to expect and to "just live with." While tolerable, they can wear you down and wipe you out. They can discourage you and cloud your sense of well-being.

It is helpful to recognize the difference between acute and chronic symptoms. Acute symptoms require action. Your body is telling you very strongly that something is not right. Tolerating or ignoring acute symptoms would not be wise; rather, seeking medical assistance, taking medication, or both would be in order. On the other hand, chronic symptoms lend themselves to a more passive response, such as mindfully bringing awareness to the body sensations and to the associated mental stories. The practices described in this book can help you to discern acute symptoms from chronic symptoms and to recognize the most appropriate and skillful response.

You Are Not Your Pain

Sometimes it is hard to separate yourself from pain and other discomforts you may experience. The sensations and associated stories consume you, and you lose perspective.

Learning to tune in can help you to develop qualities of observing and gaining perspective. With practice you can tease apart the unpleasant sensations; your impulses, judgments, and stories about them; and your sense of identity that has been subsumed in the experience. You begin to realize that you are not the pain (or any other discomfort) or just a patient or a disease—that there is much more that makes you who you are.

Turning Toward, Not Resisting

The notion of turning toward discomfort seems counterintuitive. A natural reaction is to resist it, push it away, or run away from it. The truth is, these approaches are constrictive and take mental and physical energy. And while distracting yourself from unpleasantness may seem helpful in the short run, it doesn't allow you to actually learn how to live *with* what is happening.

Interestingly enough, you may also notice that when you try to ignore something or push it away, it actually seems to have a large and unrelenting presence. Then when you turn toward and pay attention to the discomfort, it loses power over you. Sometimes by simply directing your attention toward the pain or other difficult feeling, and breathing in and out of that area of the body, you can actually dissolve the unpleasant sensations. This process also allows you to be in control so that you can do something about it, such as change your position, take medication, or redirect your attention to something neutral or pleasant. You learn that you have choices concerning how to deal with it. By turning toward the disagreeable feeling, you may also notice that it is not as bad as you had imagined it might be, which can be a profound realization.

It's of note that this practice of *turning toward* is appropriate for chronic, mild-to-moderate symptoms, as described earlier. Acute symptoms that are severe and intense would be better served by distraction or action, like getting help or taking medication.

~ MEDITATION PRACTICE ~
Body-Scan Meditation

The body-scan meditation is an excellent way to learn to tune in to and befriend your body. It involves developing awareness by slowly, gently, and systematically scanning the different regions of your body. It helps to cultivate attention skills, the flexibility to be with whatever you are feeling, and self-acceptance.

- Begin with a receptive and curious attitude. Notice any preconceived notions of what you think you will experience during or after the body scan, and see if it's possible to be present to them without believing them. Even if you've done the body scan many times before, your body, state of mind, and environment are not exactly the same as any time before.

- Notice if you are trying to force yourself to feel a certain way or if you want to *get* something out of this experience. This is a normal feeling, but it may get in the way of experiencing your body just as it is.

- Maintain awareness moment by moment as you bring your attention to different parts of your body, with the quality of your attention being to just feel what you feel.

- Be aware of whether you have resistance to bringing awareness to your body. If you do, simply notice the resistance and the sensations, thoughts, or emotions associated with it. Notice if you are judging yourself. Practice being aware, and then allow and breathe into the resistance.

- Allow yourself to settle into a comfortable position, lying down or in another position in which you feel supported and relaxed. Be in a position that supports you yet allows you to stay awake. You may choose to cover yourself with a blanket, because body temperature often drops when the body is still for a period of time.

- When you are ready, close your eyes or keep them slightly open with a soft gaze.

- Rest for a few moments in awareness of the natural rhythm of your breathing.

- Once your body and mind are settled, bring awareness to your body as a whole. Be aware of your body resting and being supported by the mattress, floor, or chair.

- The body scan generally follows this sequence: Begin with the toes of your left foot. Then shift your awareness to the different parts of your left foot (sole, heel, and top of foot), moving up through your left leg to your pelvis, down to your right toes, up through your right foot and leg, and back to your pelvis. Then bring awareness to your abdomen, lower back, upper back, chest, and shoulders; to both arms, down to your fingers; and back to your shoulders. Bring your awareness from your shoulders to your neck, and then to the different regions of your face and head. Finally, bring awareness to your body as a whole.

- For each part of your body, notice the different sensations: the quality, intensity, and constancy. Try to be aware of what you are actually feeling, such as warmth, tingling, aching, or dullness. Be open to the possibility of not feeling any sensations in some parts of your body; that's very common and completely okay.

- Linger in each area of your body for a few moments and imagine breathing into the area of attention. One option is to imagine breathing in feelings of vitality, energy, and healing; and breathing out tension, fatigue, or angst. Breathe into and out of each region a few times.

- As you linger in each part of the body, tune in to any sensations you are experiencing, including their subtle qualities. Notice if they are constant, if they wax and wane, or if they dissolve completely. You may notice that the sensations change from moment to moment or from one region of the body to the other. You may find that some sensations are pleasant, some are neutral, and some are unpleasant or uncomfortable.

- Allow thoughts or emotions to arise without pushing them away or holding on to them. Simply observe them with curiosity, rather than getting caught up in or trying to judge or interpret them. The moment you catch yourself in a judgment (like *I shouldn't be feeling this way* or *I'm not doing this right*), mental story, memory, or unrelated thought, simply pause. Acknowledge that your mind is off doing its familiar tricks; you may even smile and say to yourself something like, *Isn't it interesting that I was thinking of that?* The moment you catch your mind drifting is a wonderful reminder to re-center yourself, take a breath, and return your attention to the part of the body you last remember.

- If you fall asleep during the body scan, be kind to yourself. Your mind and body let go enough to drift off and give you needed rest and recuperation. The intention of this practice is that you do not fall asleep, although it is perfectly okay if you do. The moment you catch yourself in a stupor, take a deep breath to reawaken your body, reposition your body if necessary (which may help to wake it up), and, when you are ready, return your attention to the part of the body you last remember.

- If there is any particular part of your body that is uncomfortable and grabs your attention, allow your attention to be in that place. Do not try to ignore it. Bring awareness to the unpleasant sensations. You may also want to imagine breathing into and out of them. Notice if the discomfort lessens. If you need to, mindfully reposition your body into a more comfortable position. Then resume the body scan, returning to whatever part of the body you were focused on.

⌐ REFLECTIVE WRITING ⌐
Tuning In

To begin this writing practice, allow your mind and body to settle by taking a moment to bring your attention to the natural rhythm of your breathing. Then, when you feel centered, read each of the following questions, quietly tune in to your body, and write down your response:

- *In this moment, how am I feeling?*

- *What am I feeling? What physical sensations are present in me right now? Are they pleasant or unpleasant?*

- *What are the qualities of the sensations? Do the sensations change from moment to moment?*

- *What thoughts (stories, judgments, memories, fantasies, and so on) come to mind as I bring attention to the sensations?*

- *What emotions arise?*
- *Do I have impulses to automatically reject or embrace certain sensations? If yes, how?*
- *What insights have I gained about myself in response to this practice of tuning in to my body?*
- *Now, as I complete this writing practice, how do I feel in this moment?*

Each Day...

- Throughout the day, do mini body scans by pausing physically and mentally and tuning in to how your body is feeling.
- Catch yourself whenever your mind automatically reacts to specific body sensations by judging or creating stories.

Keep in Mind

Tuning in, as cultivated through body-scan practice, is an entry into understanding and befriending your body, and accepting it as it is right now, which allows for a larger sense of acceptance. It is an opportunity for you to be conscious of what is right or healthy in your body and to realize that all of you is *not* broken. Seeing sensations as mere sensations, and noticing their nuanced qualities and fluctuations, gives them less power.

Here are some tips for practicing the body scan: Try to do some version of the body scan at least four times every week. Take your time with this practice. It is best to not rush, and to slowly and thoughtfully explore each part of your body. The full body scan takes approximately forty-five minutes. If you don't have the time or energy to do the full body scan, then choose one part of your body, like your limbs or even just one arm or hand. If you have a tendency to fall asleep during the body scan, do this practice at a time when you have the most energy, like earlier in the day.

3

~

UNHELPFUL THOUGHTS AND OVERWHELMING EMOTIONS

Whoever can see through all fear
will always be safe.

—Tao Te Ching

After many years of living with HIV, Maggie experienced her disease progressing to a more serious stage where she was diagnosed with AIDS. Even though she was mobile and felt relatively well, the same story played over and over in Maggie's mind. She pictured herself completely debilitated and dependent on others. Each time this image filled her mind, she was overcome by feelings of deep sadness, intense fear of uncertainties in her future, and regret for events in the past. Her chest and throat would tighten, and her stomach would cramp. She'd then find herself curled up in a fetal position for hours, sobbing and shaking.

Maggie's experience is not unusual for many people living with a serious illness. Unhelpful thoughts can creep into your mind at any moment, spiral out of control, and take on a life of their own. They can pervade your life at a cost to your sense of well-being and make you squander your precious time.

Being aware of such thoughts and their insidious effect on how you feel emotionally and physically is the first step in lessening their power over you.

Unhelpful Thoughts

It is common to go about your life ruminating about the past and pondering possibilities or planning for the future. The mind does this automatically: you may not even be aware of what you are thinking about, what you are doing, or how you feel when you are carried away by your thoughts. While some thoughts can be helpful by encouraging you to be proactive and prepared, or to have a context for your current experiences, it's important to recognize that some thoughts can make you feel worse. A few common categories of *unhelpful thoughts* are dwelling in the past, worrying, having expectations, and focusing on others' expectations and reactions. Such thoughts are problematic because they can overwhelm you, drain you, and chew up precious time. They interfere with your ability to find satisfaction and live fully now.

Dwelling in the Past

Two general ways to dwell in the past are to cling to the "good ole days" and to have regrets. Being preoccupied with memories of when you were younger, with a stronger and healthier body, can make you feel uneasy about your current state, your body, and your circumstances. Yearning for the life you once had separates you from what is happening now, and it makes it harder for you to accept and be at peace with what is. You may have regret both for things you've done and for things you haven't done. While regret can inspire positive actions, like mending broken relationships, lamenting without taking action only detracts from your making *this* moment as good as it can be.

PAUSE NOW: Reflect now on whether you spend time dwelling in the past, either by wishing to return to the way things used to be or by having regrets.

Worrying

It's inevitable that as you live with an incurable illness, you will think about how the illness will progress and affect how you feel and function. It's also normal to think about what will happen to your loved ones. You might think about how your experience will affect them as you become frail and eventually die. Having concern, such as parental concern about a child's welfare, and being realistic about known circumstances can be extremely useful. It can foster proactive planning, allow you to make arrangements that are consistent with your values, and engage in important conversations. However, worrying is subtly different. It is an ungrounded and exaggerated speculation of what may come. There is a ruminative quality to worrying that is often associated with anticipation of the worst possible scenario or excessive fuss over trivial details.

PAUSE NOW: Reflect for a moment on whether you worry about the future and exaggerate what may happen to the point where the worry is no longer grounded in what is known.

Your Expectations

In spite of planning and your best efforts, circumstances may not turn out the way you had envisioned. This is because many factors influence how things unfold, and many of the factors are beyond your control. For example, you may expect your family to be supportive all of the time, but they're not. Or you may have diligently followed the treatment plan, yet your disease contin-ues to worsen. It's reasonable to have some expectations of what might hap-pen, especially if you have been conscientious in how you've approached your situation. Nevertheless, these thoughts become unhelpful—leading to disappointment, discouragement, and despair—when you are unable to accept outcomes that are different from what you had anticipated.

PAUSE NOW: Reflect now on whether you had a hard time when things turned out differently than you had expected.

Focusing on Others' Expectations and Reactions

Similarly, other people may have expectations about you. They may have trouble accepting your decisions and actions, or they may have a tough time accepting when things turn out differently than they'd like. They may react strongly and be upset, which in turn may make you feel unsettled. You may even blame yourself for their reactions, and such self-deprecating thoughts can wear you down. As with concern versus worrying, being considerate of others' expectations is appropriate. However, being preoccupied with others' expectations and reactions can make you lose your equilibrium and sense of self. In essence you waste valuable time, since you are pulled from attending to your own needs and living in a way that nourishes you.

PAUSE NOW: Reflect for a moment on how you are affected by others' expectations and reactions to what is happening with you.

Overwhelming Emotions

Emotions bring richness to your experiences, whether they uplift you or bring you down. They fluctuate in response to what you are thinking about, how your body is feeling, and your circumstances. Some emotions have positive, beneficial qualities that promote peace of mind or selfless caring for others, such as happiness or altruistic love. Other emotions have negative, destructive qualities that agitate the mind or hurt others, like anxiety or anger. It's healthy to be in touch with and to express your emotions constructively but not overly identify with them. If you excessively identify with emotions, they can overwhelm you like a tidal wave, to the point of immobilizing you, drowning you, or knocking you over. It's as if the emotion becomes one with you. As a result, it's hard for you to think clearly, experience other mental states, or notice what is happening around you. Three particularly challenging emotions for people with serious illness are fear, sadness, and anger.

Fear

Fear can involve being afraid of the unknown: What will it be like when you get sicker? How will you die? What will happen to you when you die? No matter what you fear, fear can freeze you or propel you to run away from living now.

PAUSE NOW: Reflect for a moment now on whether you experience fear, and if you do, consider what you are afraid of.

Sadness

Sadness is accompanied by a heavy heart. It is driven by a sense of longing and by actual or anticipated losses, such as loss of independence or leaving your family. Sadness can cloud your days, making it difficult for light, clarity, and joy to shine through.

PAUSE NOW: Reflect for a moment now on whether you experience sadness, and if you do, try to recognize what saddens you.

Anger

Anger is triggered by a threat to the self or ego and is associated with a sense of being on guard, attacked, or wounded. It can lead to hatred, bitterness, resentment, or hostility. Regardless of whether anger is directed toward yourself or others, it can tear you apart inside and distance you from others.

PAUSE NOW: Reflect for a moment now on whether you experience anger, and if you do, try to recognize what is contributing to your feeling angry.

Linking Thoughts, Emotions, and Bodily Sensations

If you pay close attention, you will notice that what you think about affects how you feel emotionally and how your body feels. Also, how you feel emotionally (your mood) can trigger a cascade of thoughts and bodily sensations. Likewise, how your body feels can give rise to thoughts and emotions, as with feeling a pain in your body and then automatically thinking that the illness is progressing, which in turn makes you feel very sad.

To further illustrate this connection, bring to mind an image of something that is or has been pleasurable for you, like a smiling baby or a beautiful sunset. Notice how you feel. What is your mood? Perhaps happy? How does your body feel? Perhaps energized or relaxed?

The reason for this connection among your thoughts, emotions, and bodily sensations is that the wiring within the brain is intricately connected and also integrated with the rest of the body. The thinking part of the brain (the *cortex*) and the emotion part of the brain (the *limbic system*) continually communicate back and forth. Additionally, the brain is anatomically connected to the rest of the body through nerves and blood vessels, so thoughts and emotions affect the way your body feels and vice versa. The bottom line is that there is a dynamic interplay among your thoughts, emotions, and bodily sensations and functioning. It makes sense that taming your thoughts can make your emotions less overwhelming and ultimately enhance how your body feels and increase your overall sense of well-being.

Easing the Grip of Disruptive Thoughts and Emotions

Disruptive thoughts and emotions can have power over you. If you allow them to have a tight hold on you, they will throw you around and beat you up. Understanding the root of your thoughts and emotions and learning to simply observe and not overly identify with them is essential to loosening their grip and lessening their power over you.

We have all faced adversities in our lives. Some of them appeared quite threatening at the time. As we look back over time, the same events aren't frightening, because time enables us to view them more objectively.

Simply Observing

Thoughts and emotions are mental events that come and go. They do not have any more of a tangible form than a cloud does. You can see a cloud, yet if you try to grab a cloud, your hands will come up empty. In this way, thoughts and emotions are not solid.

An important aspect of not getting caught up in thoughts or emotions is to be an impartial witness, observing their coming and going like clouds moving across the sky. Simply observing creates distance so that these mental states are not so overwhelming. It also brings understanding so that you can realize their causes and consequences.

As described earlier, thoughts and emotions often occur in tandem and can stimulate or attenuate each other. In his book *Why Meditate?* Matthieu Ricard, a Buddhist monk and trained scientist, describes the emotion of anger as akin to a fire in a fireplace (Ricard 2010). If you simply watch the fire and notice its qualities, like warmth, colors, and light, and do not add any wood, the fire will cool down and eventually go out. The fire is like emotions (anger in this example), and the wood is like thoughts that fuel the emotion (for example, mentally replaying the story of someone doing you wrong). If you stop the story or memories, then the emotion will gradually fade and eventually go away.

Naming Your Thoughts and Emotions

Another way to let go of challenging thoughts and emotions is by recognizing and naming them, such as "memory," "planning," "worrying," or "idea." So often, people want to push away or suppress mental or emotional experiences. However, you need to "name it to tame it," according to psychiatrist and author Dan Siegel (Boyce 2011). Research supports this notion, of naming or labeling disturbing thoughts and emotions (Creswell et al. 2007). It helps you to break free from the rut of rumination.

Redirecting and Counteracting Thoughts

You can also intentionally redirect your attention to something neutral or positive, or you can counteract worrisome thoughts with wholesome images or aspirations for goodness for self and others. These approaches can be particularly helpful if it's too uncomfortable or unsettling to observe the thoughts or emotions that challenge you. For example, if you are worrying about what may happen and you're feeling scared, you can shift your attention to something right in front of you, like looking out the window and up at the sky. Or if you are thinking about how someone has hurt you and you're feeling sad or angry, you can imagine that you are both wounded, then quietly contemplate good wishes for healing and love to both of you.

Nonjudging

Part of growing up is learning to think critically and analytically. Our minds are conditioned to judge, meaning we automatically evaluate our own experiences and others' experiences without being conscious of it. Judging just happens, like a reflex, and it happens all the time throughout the day. Judging can interfere with our ability to be objective and can prevent us from fully experiencing what is actually happening.

The key to nonjudging is learning to be an impartial observer or witness of your thoughts and experiences. In the following practices, you should just notice thoughts as thoughts and events as events. It's also important that you don't judge the judging, meaning not being critical of yourself when you catch yourself judging.

~ MEDITATION PRACTICE ~
Observing Thoughts

- After settling into a comfortable position, either lying down or sitting, notice the sensations of your breathing, as described in the previous chapters. Simply pay attention to the natural rhythm of breathing in and breathing out.

- Whenever you find that your mind has wandered off the sensations of breathing to thinking, turn your attention toward the thought.

  - Notice the thought, and note the story that is playing in your mind.

  - Try to just watch it as a neutral yet interested observer, as if you were watching a movie. Or, imagine a pane of glass separating you from your thoughts.

  - Describe what you see (what you are thinking about). Whom and what do you see? What's happening?

  - Name the thought: a "memory," "plan," "fantasy," "random idea," or some other kind of thought.

  - Notice the thought as it drifts out of your mind, like a cloud that floats across the sky and disappears from your field of awareness.

- Return your awareness to the sensations of breathing.

- When you catch yourself in thought again, turn your attention to the thought and follow the sequence described previously: notice the thought, observe it, describe it, and name it. Then return to the experience of breathing.

Thinking and Feeling

- As you prepare to write, pause for a moment to notice what thoughts come to mind. Thoughts can be very simple and superficial, like *This chair is comfortable,* or more involved, like *I'm worried about my son.*

- Whatever you are thinking about at this time, just begin writing about it. Write for three to five minutes about whatever comes to mind. You may write about the same thought that you started with or new thoughts that may or may not be related to it. After a few minutes, stop writing and just pause.

- Notice whatever emotions you are experiencing. You may notice for example happiness, sadness, or indifference (meaning you have no particular feelings). Write for a few minutes about the feelings you're experiencing. Stop writing and pause again.

- Tune in to your body (as described in the previous chapter) and notice any physical sensations that you feel (if any). Then write for a few minutes about these bodily sensations and how your body is feeling in general (calm, tense, relaxed, and so on).

- Finally, consider what new insights you may have gained about your thoughts, emotions, and bodily sensations. If you like, take a few minutes to write about what you've learned about yourself through this writing practice.

Each Day...

Pause periodically and become aware of what you are thinking about. Notice how the thoughts may affect your emotions and your body.

Keep in Mind

Unhelpful thoughts and overwhelming emotions can have power over you, at a cost to your sense of well-being, and can dissipate precious time and energy. What you think about affects how you feel, emotionally and physically. Learning to recognize and observe your thoughts without overly identifying with them will lessen their control and bring greater balance to your life.

4

〜

LISTENING AND LOOKING: INSIDE AND OUTSIDE

The voyage of discovery is not in seeking new landscapes, but in having new eyes.

—Marcel Proust, *La Prisonnière*

It's very common to feel as if your world has gotten smaller, more closed in, and more constricted as a result of your illness. You may spend less time outdoors and more time confined to the house or hospital. Even if you are able to get out and about, you may be so consumed with your internal world—your body and thoughts—that you don't even really notice the immediate world around you, inside and outside of your living space. Or you may deliberately shut out what's happening around you, since you may not like where you are and wish deep down that you were somewhere else.

For many years I have worked with people with serious illnesses, including cancer patients undergoing bone-marrow transplant. As a nurse and researcher on the bone-marrow transplant unit, I have witnessed the challenges of these patients who are hospitalized with isolation precautions for three or more weeks at a time. They generally don't want to be in the hospital, especially for so long. Besides not feeling well and being away from loved ones, they simply find it an unpleasant place to be, despite the hospital staff's best intentions. The hospital environment is filled with beeping machines, constant interruptions at all hours of the day and night, foul and sterile hospital smells, and an uncomfortable bed. Enduring this environment for weeks is hard for nearly everyone.

Recognizing these challenges, my colleagues and I have adapted and brought mindfulness practices to hospitalized patients. One practice we have found to be especially helpful involves auditory and visual awareness. Anyone who feels trapped inside the body or confined to a limited living space might benefit from this practice of intentionally paying attention to sounds and sights. As with other attention practices already discussed, this practice promotes a stable mind. However, it also fosters a sense of spaciousness, and an acceptance of and appreciation for your immediate surroundings, as well as a connection to the outside environment.

Noticing Sounds

At any given time there are a number of different sounds in your environment. However, you likely notice just one or two of the loudest or most compelling sounds. And even for those sounds that you obviously hear, like someone talking to you, there's a good chance that you aren't really aware of the qualities of the sounds, how they resonate in your body, or how they affect your mood.

As we explore awareness of sound, consider the following questions: What is your relationship to sound? Are you an auditory learner, meaning you learn best by hearing things? Do you like to have a lot of simultaneous sounds humming all around you, or do you prefer silence? Are there times when you like it noisy and other times when quiet feels right for you? How do different sounds affect your emotions and the way your body feels? What sounds are comforting to you? How do you know they make you feel good—where in your body do you feel it? Conversely, what sounds are unpleasant to you? What about them is disagreeable, and where in your body do you feel it? In general what thoughts (for example, memories, fantasies, or conceptions) come to mind when you hear different sounds? Do you have trouble hearing, are you hypersensitive to sounds, or do you have ringing in your ears? If so, what feelings arise when you consider or face your hearing challenges?

Reflect for a moment on all of the different sounds co-occurring around you at this time: the sounds in the room where you are, the sounds in the building but outside of your room, or the sounds outside. Inside you may hear talking, laughter, footsteps, water running, music, or electronic appliances, to name a few. Or if you listen more closely, you may notice a clock ticking, a cat purring, or the vibratory humming of the heater or air conditioner. Outside sounds you may notice are rain falling, wind blowing, cars going by, dogs barking, and birds and crickets chirping.

The number of sounds accessible to you in any given moment can be vast. You have the ability to consciously expand your field of awareness to an array of different sounds. You can scan the different sounds around you, and then choose to focus on particular sounds that are pleasant and make you feel good. It may be the sound of gentle rain on the roof that washes away your worries or the quiet ticking of the clock that makes you feel centered. It may be a sound you hadn't really heard before or ever noticed how it made you feel. With attention you may now realize that certain sounds make you feel happy, energized, or relaxed, while other sounds make you feel tense, sad, or agitated. The practice of awareness of sound grounds you in your direct experiences in the present moment through your sense of hearing. It helps you to discern different sounds available to you at any moment and how they make you feel. You can thoughtfully shift your awareness toward sounds that engender a sense of well-being, and you can turn away from or tune out sounds that bring unease.

~ MEDITATION PRACTICE ~
Listening Inside and Outside

- Allow yourself to settle into a comfortable position, either lying down or sitting, and bring awareness to your chest and abdomen, expanding with each inbreath and contracting with each outbreath.

- Once your mind and body are settled, move your awareness from your breathing to sounds. If you'd like, you may close your eyes. By closing your eyes, you may be better able to pay attention to sound.

- Scan your field of awareness for sounds close to you in the room. Notice what sounds immediately catch your attention.

- Try focusing now on just one sound.

  - Notice the qualities of the sound: the tone, pitch, loudness, and rhythm.

  - As you listen to the sound, tune in to your body, noticing if you can feel the sound resonating in your body; if so, where do you feel it?

  - Notice thoughts or feelings that may arise as you attend to the sound. Be aware if you start to get carried away with stories surrounding the sound. If that occurs, simply acknowledge that your mind has wandered, and come back to noticing the qualities of the sound.

  - When you are ready, move your awareness to another sound close to you. Notice the qualities of this sound, where you feel it in your body, and if associated thoughts and emotions arise.

- Explore all sounds in your immediate vicinity in this way.

- Then expand your field of awareness to other sounds in the building. Notice all of the different sounds: voices, movements, appliances or technology, music, pets, and so on. What are all of the different sounds you can hear right now?

- What are the qualities of the different sounds?

- Bring awareness to how your body feels as you listen to the different sounds.

- Notice your thoughts and feelings as you scan the different sounds inside the house or building.

- After you have thoroughly explored the different sounds inside, you can now expand your awareness to the sounds outside. Notice the different kinds of sounds outside, like rain falling or wind blowing; different modes of transportation, such as cars, trucks, trains, and airplanes; people talking; dogs barking; birds chirping; and so on. Perhaps it is very quiet, and you don't think you hear anything. Allow yourself to be still and to really pay attention to subtle sounds or the lack of sound.

  - Try not to get caught up in the stories surrounding the sounds or what the sounds mean, but listen to the essence of the sounds.

  - Be aware of how the sounds affect your body or how they do not affect it.

  - Notice thoughts, such as memories, plans, or conceptions, that may arise in response to particular sounds.

  - Notice emotions that surface in response to certain sounds.

  - Try to keep your focus on the qualities of sound, the changes in sound from one moment to the next, and the silence between the sounds.

- After you have explored all of the different sounds outside, just allow yourself to rest for a few moments and notice how you feel right now.

What Do I Hear?

- Allow your mind and body to settle.

- Close your eyes and be aware of the sounds you hear.

- Write about your experience of attending to sounds. Try to focus on one sound at a time.

  - Focus on the qualities of the sound: the tone, pitch, loudness, and rhythm.

  - Notice if you can feel the sound resonate in your body. Where does it resonate in your body?

  - Note any thoughts (including stories or memories) or emotions that arise in response to listening to the sound.

Noticing Sights

The capacity to expand your awareness goes beyond sound. It also relates to other senses, including sight. It is common to have a narrow field of vision, not noticing all of the different sights before you. You may see only what you are looking for or hope to see, thereby missing surprises or hidden treasures. Or you may see only a small aspect of what you are looking at and miss the "big picture" of what is before you. Or you may have an idea or mental construction of what you are seeing, rather than noticing the qualities of what you're actually seeing.

Just as we explored with sound, consider the following questions with regard to visual awareness: What is your relationship to sight? Are you a visual learner, meaning you learn best by seeing things? What do you notice about colors, light, shadows, shapes, and spatiality? Are you drawn to particular visual experiences depending on your mood? How does what you see affect your mood? What colors, light, and space elements are comforting to you? How do you know they make you feel good—where in your body do you feel it? On the other hand, what images or qualities of your visual experiences are not pleasant to you? What is it about them that is unappealing, and where in your body do you feel it? In general, what thoughts (memories, fantasies, or conceptions) arise when you see different things? Do you have trouble seeing? If so, what feelings arise when you consider or face your vision challenges?

The variety of colors, shades, light, shadows, and shapes that could be brought into your field of awareness from one moment to the next is limitless. You can intentionally scan your visual field of awareness and choose to expand the scope of what you see or to focus on particular images. You may choose to notice things that make you feel alive or more in touch with your feelings, like white, puffy clouds floating across the wide, blue sky; the dark and sincere eyes of your beloved dog; or raindrops slowly gliding down the window. Or you may notice something that you hadn't really seen before or hadn't been aware of how it made you feel. As you pay attention to what you see, you can recognize how certain things that you see make you feel joyful, rejuvenated, or calm; and others make you feel anxious, gloomy, or angry. You'll also see that you can shift your visual awareness at will.

In his book *Selfless Insight: Zen and the Meditative Transformations of Consciousness*, pioneering neurologist James Austin (2009) describes how different parts of the brain and body are activated depending on where and at what the eyes are looking. (His book *Meditating Selflessly: Practical Neural Zen* [forthcoming] covers this subject in even greater detail.) For example, if you look down or straight in front of you at inanimate objects, then you will likely enter a more self-focused and discursive frame of mind. On the other hand, if you allow your eyes to effortlessly drift upward to see the leaves on the trees, the clouds in the sky, or the stars at night, you are more likely to be receptive and experience a feeling of openness, and to sense it in your body. Furthermore, recent exploration in this area has identified benefits of gazing upward in people who have experienced a trauma. In certain people, gazing upward while revisualizing the traumatic episode enables the person to dissolve the emotional burden associated with that trauma (Austin, personal communication).

PAUSE NOW: Experiment by looking straight or down at an object and then receptively gazing out the window up at the tree-tops and the sky. As you look in different directions, tune in and notice how your body feels.

◁ MEDITATION PRACTICE ▷
Looking Inside and Outside

- Position yourself in such a way that you can look around the room yet easily also look out the window or door.

- Allow yourself to get settled into a comfortable position. You may begin by closing your eyes and tuning in to the natural rhythm of your breathing.

- Once you are settled, open your eyes. Without moving your head, begin by noticing the light, colors, and shapes as you open your eyes.

- Gently and slowly scan the room, and first notice colors.

  - Notice all of the different colors and shades of color.

  - Be aware of how your body and mind feel as you look at the different colors.

- Move your awareness to light and shadows.

- Then notice the different shapes.

- Allow yourself to explore and really settle into the experience of noticing light, shadows, and shapes. What do you notice?

  - Try not to get caught up in the stories of what the images mean or represent.

  - Try to stay with the qualities or essence of what you are seeing.

- Now bring your awareness to space—the space between objects or rooms—and notice how your body and mind feel as you explore this sense of space.

- After you have thoroughly explored the visual experience inside the room, turn your head and body to face outside.

  - Allow yourself to scan your visual field of awareness outside. Explore color, shades of color, light and shadows, shapes, and space. What do you notice?

  - How does your body feel when you look at different things outside?

  - Are there memories or plans that come to mind?

  - What emotions are you feeling, if any?

  - If you find your mind running off into an elaborate story, acknowledge it with curiosity (such as, *Oh, isn't that interesting?*), and then come back to the act of seeing colors, light, shapes, and so on.

  - Try to keep this very simple.

- After you have looked around outside very carefully and completely, close your eyes and allow yourself to just sit quietly for a few moments, and notice how you feel right now.

～ REFLECTIVE WRITING ～
What Do I See?

- Allow your mind and body to settle, and for a few moments close your eyes or keep them open with a soft, unfocused gaze.

- Open your eyes or sharpen your focus to notice what you see. You may choose to begin by looking up.

- Write about what you see.

  - Note the qualities of what you see: the colors or shades of color, light and shadows, shapes, and the sense of space.

- Describe how your body feels when you look at what's in your field of vision.
- Comment on any thoughts or emotions you may have as you look at what is in your field of vision.

Vivid and Spacious Awareness

When you develop the capacity to listen and see mindfully, you will notice how the world around you takes on a different perspective. Two qualities emerge: vividness and spaciousness. The opposite of dullness, *vividness* corresponds to a deepening and enriching of your experiences through a sharpening of your senses. It creates a feeling of vibrancy that results in ordinary experiences having greater meaning. *Spaciousness* is the opposite of feeling cramped. Here, it relates to a sense of expansiveness brought about by an awareness of the range of sounds and sights available to you in any given moment. You can move out of feeling confined, like a hostage to bodily limitations and circumstances, and move toward the infinite possibilities of experiences accessible to you right now.

～ Julie's Story: Clocks Ticking, Trees Swaying

Julie, a forty-six-year-old, married mother of two young daughters, had recurrent leukemia and was in the hospital for extensive treatment that was expected to last several weeks. She missed her family and her home. She absolutely hated being there and essentially wanted to sleep through the whole hospitalization. She was bored by the monotony of her days and the sterile off-white hospital room, and she was frustrated by the constant interruptions. She was so preoccupied with how bad she felt that fears and stories of the worst-case scenario filled her mind. Whenever Julie looked at the clock, she got agitated. She felt that it wasn't moving fast enough and, at the same time, had the feeling that she was running out of time. She kept the window shades drawn, since she knew she wouldn't be going outside anytime soon.

Aware of how miserable she was, Julie decided to explore mindfulness practices to try to cope better with her situation. She worked with a nurse who was skilled in teaching mindfulness, and she listened to guided meditation audio recordings. She figured it couldn't hurt and hoped it would help. With gentle guidance, she became more receptive to her surroundings. Even though Julie was in the same place with similar day-to-day routines, she started noticing things she hadn't paid attention to before, and her attitude changed from uninterested to inquisitive. Rather than push away what was happening and wish things were different, Julie gradually opened up to her experiences by listening and looking with a spirit of kindness and curiosity.

Inside the hospital room, beyond the blaring television, intercom announcements, and buzzing and beeping of high-tech machines, Julie was able to bring her attention to the background hum of the ventilation system. She was comforted by the constancy of the specialized system designed to purify the air and keep out harmful germs. She could also hear the clock. She would catch her mind in stories about what the clock represents (such as time passing slowly or running out of time) and simply come back to the sounds and movement of ticking, one second at a time. She gradually found it quite settling to listen to and watch the clock ticking. It became a neutral point of focus that she was able to synchronize with the rhythm of her breathing. She also began to notice the intravenous (IV) fluids continually dripping and flowing into her body. She recognized that she had viewed the IVs as tying her down and also a reminder of being sick. Pausing and looking at the fluid droplets allowed her to settle into the moment, one drop at a time. Eventually Julie's resistance to the IV dissolved, and she realized the life-giving intention of being connected to it. Then, when the IV machine would beep (indicating that the medication had finished running in or that it was time to change the fluid bag), rather than tense up, she used it as an opportunity to center herself, a reminder to pay attention to her breathing. Looking around her room, Julie noticed the colors of the countless cards and drawings on the windowsill and taped to the wall, and she had a revelation that filled her with boundless love: she had the deep realization that so many people cared about her and that they had taken the time to think of her and send her good wishes.

The practice of listening and looking outside was very difficult for Julie. She was overcome with sadness, because she wasn't able to be "normal" and go about living her life in as carefree of a way as the people she could see through the window. Rather than resist her sadness, she simply sat by the window and gazed out. She allowed herself to feel the sadness as the tears welled up in her eyes and tightness grabbed her throat and chest. Connecting with and breathing into the feelings, she could slowly feel them dissipate. She could then look out and see what was actually happening outside. She was drawn to the sky, with its openness, and the clouds changing shapes and moving before her. She could see birds flying and trees swaying. Seeing children playing, she found herself wondering about how her own children were managing without her, and she silently wished them well. Julie realized that by looking outside and seeing the sky, birds, and trees, she had connected with nature, which had always been a source of strength for her. Her mind felt wider and freer. She was comforted by the awareness that the world goes on and that in some ways, however small, she continued to be part of the whole.

PAUSE NOW: Pause now and notice how you feel after reading Julie's story. What do you notice in your body? What thoughts and feelings are you experiencing right now? What aspect of Julie's story touched a chord in you? What could you relate to and what couldn't you relate to? Simply pause and check in with what is true for you right now.

Each Day...

- At least once a day, stop what you are doing or thinking, close your eyes, and listen to sounds. See if you can discern the different sounds you hear, all occurring at the same time. Be aware of whatever comes up for you as you bring your attention to the sounds.

- Take a few moments to be outside and to look up. If you are not able to go outside, then look out the window or door. Look up and connect with nature, noticing such things as the color of the sky, the movement and shape of clouds, the stars and moon, trees swaying, the color of the leaves, birds, butterflies, raindrops or snowflakes, and light and shadows.

Keep in Mind

In every moment there are countless sounds and sights all around, but you may rarely hear or see what is available to you. It is possible to intentionally bring attention to different sounds and sights, and then notice how your body and mind respond. The practice of mindfully attending to sounds and sights will bring more vividness to your experiences and give you a feeling of spaciousness and connectedness with the world around you.

5

~

EVERYDAY ACTIVITIES AND ACCEPTING CHANGES

Let the beauty we love be what we do.
There are a hundred ways to kneel and kiss the ground.

—Rumi, *The Essential Rumi*

Many of us go through each day on automatic pilot, rolling out of bed and proceeding without any awareness of what we're doing. We are lost in thought—planning, worrying, regretting, fantasizing, or solving the problems of the world—all at the same time while we brush our teeth. As you go about your day *doing* things, are you aware of the actual experience of what you're doing? Simple and ordinary daily activities—like eating, walking, washing your face, and taking medication—are all opportunities to ground yourself in present-moment awareness. You don't need to do anything special or go anywhere exotic.

In my work teaching mindfulness to patients in the hospital, I often suggest that when the alarm on the intravenous machine sounds (indicating that the medication has finished or that the fluid bag needs to be changed), they stay present with the experience. Rather than stop or take a break from the meditation practice, or ignore the ringing, they are instructed to integrate the sounds and the related experience into their field of awareness: to notice the qualities (tone, rate, and volume) of the sound, to notice the presence of the nurse addressing the issue with the machine, and to notice thoughts (like *I wonder what this sound means* or *When will the nurse be done?*) and reactions (like feeling tense or annoyed). This is an example of how real-life interruptions can become part of the practice.

The alarming of machines or the beeping of computers in the hospital or in our homes is quite common, occurring several times a day. Over the course of the day, every time the machine or computer sounds, you could use it as a reminder to pause and settle into the sensations of breathing and notice what you're doing, what you're thinking about, and how you are feeling. Consider the various ordinary, everyday sounds and events that could serve as reminders to drop into the present moment, such as the ringing of the telephone or doorbell and the beep of an e-mail notification.

Being present while you engage in everyday activities doesn't mean you will necessarily find pleasure in them. Sometimes you may sense enjoyment or satisfaction, and other times you may not. You may glean new insights about yourself in the way that you see, interpret, and respond to what you're doing. Or you may notice something that you never noticed before, even though you've done the same thing a thousand times before. You may notice how the experience of a familiar activity seems different than it did before. It seems different because it is, in fact, different. No two moments are exactly the same. You are different, your awareness is different, and the circumstances are different. When you recognize that things are different, you come to appreciate change and its omnipresence and inevitability.

Indeed, change is happening around us and within us every single day, whether we are aware of it or not. I am reminded of a realization about change that occurred many years ago when I was learning to meditate. It was springtime, and I sat down in front of a bunch of newly picked daffodils. As I settled for the first few minutes, I simply observed the daffodil stems and tight buds, noticing the colors, shapes, and smell. I then softened my gaze and attended to the sensations of my breathing. About thirty minutes later, I more fully opened my eyes and expanded my field of awareness, and

I just sat there, again taking in the flowers before me. To my amazement, they were no longer tight buds. The petals were opening, the scent was stronger and sweeter, and the shades of yellow were deeper. Change was happening right before my eyes! I was awestruck. That experience led me to keenly pay attention to other changes happening, not only around me but within me. To my chagrin, I began to notice new gray hairs and new freckles when I looked in the mirror and how my body wasn't as agile as it used to be. Other changes revealed themselves in my body and in my ability to do everyday things. I also noticed my reactive aversion to the not-so-pleasant changes in my body. I learned much about myself in this self-reflection: I realized how it was hard for me to accept changes in me and my loved ones as a result of getting old and getting sick. I now know that I am not alone, because change is a challenge for everyone. How can we accept the unavoidable changes in our bodies and in our everyday lives that relate to aging and illness? We can bring awareness to our everyday activities in a way that grounds us to present-moment experience and allows us to accept the incessant changes as they unfold.

Awareness in Everyday Activities

Every activity that you partake in throughout the course of a day is an opportunity to practice being mindful. Eating, walking, and washing your face can all be done in such a way that you are aware of what you're doing and how you feel doing it.

Mindful Eating

Given the frequency with which we generally partake of food and drink throughout each day, it makes sense that mindful eating be an essential practice in cultivating mindfulness in everyday life. While eating and drinking are necessary to sustain us, these activities often have positive associations, such as pleasure in tasty food and beverages and the enjoyable social aspects surrounding meals.

For people who have a serious illness, however, eating and drinking can pose tremendous challenges, and the pleasurable aspects may be greatly diminished.

Some people who are not well don't feel like eating, because they don't have much of an appetite or they feel nauseated as a result of side effects from medication or other illness-related changes in their bodies. Taste changes are common with illness, and some foods don't seem to taste the way they used to. Some people with serious illness have a dry mouth, swallowing difficulties, or a full feeling in the belly that limits how much they are able to eat. Others may have swollen gums or throat sores that sting and burn to the point where they avoid food altogether.

If you have trouble eating as a result of your illness, eating mindfully may be helpful. Being mindful encourages you to listen to your body and to make prudent food choices that agree with your body and how you feel at the time. If you have taste changes, this is an opportunity for you to experiment with different foods and explore different flavors and textures to see what is most appealing to you. If you are unable to swallow at all, you may still experience the pleasures of taste by putting food on your lips and tongue, chewing it briefly, and then spitting into a paper napkin. And if you have mouth sores, dry mouth, or a poor appetite, you may find that mindfully taking in ice chips can be satisfying.

A friend of mine, named Elizabeth, had a progressive illness that left her with little appetite and an upset stomach. This was worsened by medications that she took to control the symptoms, which resulted in a miserably dry mouth that felt as if it were filled with cotton. She found that the simple practice of mindfully eating ice chips was settling and satisfying. She was aware of bringing each ice chip to her lips, feeling the coolness, then gradually putting the chip in her mouth, feeling it melt in her mouth and then slide down her throat. This practice of eating one ice chip at a time settled her mind and stomach, moistened her mouth, and satisfied her thirst.

Eating can be emotionally charged, because it is intertwined with pleasure, socialization, and memories. Because of the social side of eating and because food often represents how people express love to one another in many cultures, the issue of eating (or not) can get sticky for those living with serious illness. It may bring you closer to your loved ones, or it may become a wedge between you. If eating is difficult for you, you may tend to withdraw from social situations and feel frustrated, because you wish you were able to eat or because family and friends keep urging you to join them in eating. While you know their pressure comes from good intentions, it may make you more withdrawn or lead you to lash out at your loved ones, which you could later regret. Mindfulness practice may help you to open up to and ease into the social aspects of eating. You can bring awareness to your loved ones' good intentions of preparing and cooking your favorite foods. Rather than lash out, you can convey love and appreciation to them, even if you are not able to eat what they've prepared for you.

> **PAUSE NOW:** Be aware of how you feel right now. What emotions and bodily sensations are true for you at this time as you consider your loved ones and issues related to eating?

Despite the many possible challenges people with life-limiting illness face, mindful eating (and drinking) can be a positive and powerful daily practice. It involves paying attention to different tastes, smells, sounds (like crunching), and touch sensations (such as temperatures and textures in the mouth and on the lips); and doing so in a receptive, inquisitive, and gentle way. Since eating (or being unable to eat) will likely bring up strong emotions, the practice of mindful eating is a wonderful opportunity to learn about yourself, including any automatic reactions you may have to pleasantness *and* unpleasantness around the eating experience. You can gain further insights by noticing how you naturally associate certain foods with memories of significant occasions and special people and places. These associations stem from the fact that the areas in the brain associated with smell and taste are wired closely with its memory regions.

Mindful eating may also include awareness and gratitude for how the food was grown or made and how you are interconnected with nature and with distant strangers who had a hand in the long trail of production leading to the food's ending up on your plate and in your mouth. For example, consider fresh blueberries in your breakfast bowl: the sun, rain, and nutrients in the soil nourished the bushes; farmers tended them and picked the berries;

65

someone washed, packaged, and transported the berries to your local market; your good friend who knew how much you love blueberries bought them at the market; and in the morning your spouse prepared them in a lovely pottery bowl and brought them to you for you to savor and be nourished.

~ MEDITATION PRACTICE ~
Mindful Eating

Choose a food that you like and that you know your body can tolerate. If food is more than you can handle right now, then do this exercise with ice chips. Approach this practice with an attitude of curiosity, as if this is the first time you have ever eaten this food, or as if this is an experiment and you don't know what you'll find. Try taking the following steps with your eyes open and then with eyes closed, and notice the difference.

- Begin by holding the food in your hands and exploring what it feels like, noticing the temperature, texture, shape, and so on.

- Notice if it makes any sounds in your hands, from the pressure of your fingers or by shaking it.

- Smell it and be aware of the qualities of the smell (or lack of smell) and any memories associated with the scent.

- Look at it carefully. See the colors, shapes, translucency, and so on. Bring it toward the light and notice if it looks different.

- Gradually bring it (ideally a small morsel of it) toward your mouth. Do not immediately put it into your mouth. Notice saliva starting in your mouth and any reactions, such as wanting to eat it quickly.

- Allow it to rest on your lips for a few moments, noticing what it feels like on your lips and if there is any taste or smell.

- Then put the morsel into your mouth. Just hold it and move it around in your mouth for twenty seconds or longer. Notice the taste and if it changes when it moves to different parts of your tongue. Notice the texture and moisture. Notice if it begins to dissolve in your mouth or not. Chew it (if solid) thoroughly, and be aware of the process of chewing and what that feels like.

- When you are ready, swallow it. Be aware of the sensations and imagine the internal movement as it goes from the back of your throat, through the esophagus, and down into your stomach. (Note: if you are unable to swallow, be sure to spit into a napkin rather than swallow, to avoid having the food go down the airway instead of the food pipe.)

- Repeat the previous steps with the remaining food until you are finished. Do not rush. Try to stay present to the experience. See if you can notice something new each time you go through the steps.

- Notice what may be pleasant or unpleasant about the experience, and notice any tendencies to judge, want, or push away.

- Be aware of where the food came from and your connections with the natural world and all the plants, animals, and people that created the food and brought it to you.

- Engender a feeling of gratefulness throughout the experience: be grateful for your ability to eat and for the beings who have given their lives and labors so that you may eat.

Mindful Movement

Another way to bring mindfulness into everyday life is through paying attention to body movements. You can bring awareness to how you move and what it feels like to make natural body movements as you go about your day, doing things like walking or making the bed. Alternatively you can deliberately move your body with intentional awareness and an attitude of openness through gentle yoga or other mild stretching and movement activities.

Moving the body is good for you. It increases blood circulation, facilitates deeper breaths, increases energy, loosens joints, eases muscle tension, fosters flexibility, promotes skin integrity, and enhances a feeling of well-being. Most people say that they feel better, often less stressed, after walking and stretching. And, incorporating a dimension of mindful awareness adds the benefit of grounding you and making the experience more pleasurable.

Mindful Walking

There are a number of ways to bring mindfulness into walking. You can pay attention to the physical connection with the floor or ground, which in turn leads you to feel mentally grounded. If you walk slowly, you can become aware of the process of lifting each foot and placing it down. You can notice your balance: what it feels like when you are literally off balance and what supports you to regain your balance. If you walk quickly, you can be aware of your accelerated breathing and heartbeat. You can synchronize your breathing with taking steps, such as breathing in as you lift each foot up and breathing out as you place it down, which helps your mind to focus. You can also expand awareness to your surroundings while you are walking and really pay attention to the experience rather than get absorbed in thought.

~ MEDITATION PRACTICE ~
Mindful Walking

- Stand and be aware of your feet on the floor or ground. Feel the support of the earth beneath you.

- Slowly bend your left knee and lift your foot, extend the leg, and place the foot down. Notice the brief pause between steps.

- Repeat the previous sequence with your right foot and leg. Continue to pay attention to the natural rhythm of walking for a few minutes, focusing on one leg and then the other.

- Notice feelings of balance or imbalance, and notice how you stabilize and regain balance.

- Experiment with synchronizing your breath with each step: breathing in as you lift your foot up and breathing out as you place it down. Do this for a few minutes.

- Expand your awareness to your surroundings. If you are outside, observe nature, such as the sky, birds, trees, or even anthills that may be on the ground before you.

Mindful Stretching

Stretching the body gently and mindfully is the foundation of yoga, an ancient practice that literally means "union of body and mind." Many people have ideas about what yoga is, conjuring up images of trim bodies contorting into positions that are impossible for the average person to get into. While some serious yoga students and teachers indeed fit that image, there is much more to yoga that is accessible to everyone. Rather than focus on the word "yoga," I prefer to use the term *mindful stretching*, because it may dispel resistance to exploring this practice. Mindful stretching involves moving parts of your body with gentleness and awareness in a particular direction to the point where you sense your body naturally resisting, then briefly holding the position and breathing into the resistance, and finally releasing and returning to your original position. For example, you can mindfully stretch your neck (an area where most of us hold tension) by slowly and carefully dropping one ear toward the same shoulder. When it gets to the point where you cannot comfortably go further, stop and hold the position, and breathe into it for a few breaths; then release the position, return your head to center, and repeat the sequence on the other side. Notice how your body feels before you start the stretch and how it feels afterward. Mindful stretching involves tuning in and listening to your body, which means, in this regard, going only as far as feels right for you and immediately stopping if you feel pain.

Range-of-Motion Exercises

Another kind of mindful movement is the use of gentle range-of-motion exercises. Most people can do this, even those who may not be able to get out of bed. It involves simple lifting of arms and legs, and rotation of joints, like fingers, wrists, or ankles, while paying attention to the subtleties of what you are doing.

I recall spending time with a man named Jim when I was a hospice nurse. Jim was too weak to get out of bed, so we did a very gentle mindful movement practice with his hands. He looked at his palms and carefully observed the lines in his hands and the texture of his skin. He then gradually rolled one finger at a time, then unrolled one finger at a time, and quietly and rhythmically repeated the sequence several times. In the process he sensed gratitude welling up inside of him as he realized what his hands had done throughout his life: creating things in his livelihood as a carpenter, holding his daughter when she was a baby, and now tenderly clasping his wife's hand as she sat by his bedside. This simple practice became much more than just loosening his joints; it allowed Jim to focus his attention on present-moment experience while also connecting with meaningful memories.

Mindful Personal Care

Another way to bring mindfulness into your everyday life is through personal-care activities, such as taking a shower or bath, brushing your teeth or hair, shaving, rubbing lotion on your skin, and taking your medication. Essentially every day for your entire life, you have done tasks like these without awareness of the actual experience.

Consider for a moment what it's like when you take a shower: Do you feel the sensations of water running over you? Are you aware of the lather and scents of the soap and shampoo? Do they feel refreshing? How does the shower affect your energy level?

And now consider also what it's like when you take medication: Are you cognizant of why you are taking it? Are you aware of the experience of putting the medicine in your mouth and swallowing it? Are you aware of thoughts and feelings that arise as you take it, such as relief or resistance?

Personal care is a practical way for you to be kind to yourself. Treat yourself with loving attention, as you would treat those whom you love most. You, too, deserve it. The quality of attentiveness that you bring to these ordinary activities has an effect on how you feel. The more thoughtful you are when engaging in basic personal care, the more likely that you will experience pleasure and satisfaction from it.

Many people with serious illness eventually need assistance with regular personal-care activities. Whether loved ones or professionals help you, it is an opportunity for you to be receptive and to notice how they help to meet your basic needs. Allowing and not resisting others' care, such as being fully present to the experience of having skin lotion massaged into your dry hands and feet, can be relaxing and comforting.

Accepting Changes

As you age and the disease progresses, you may notice many changes in your life: the way your body feels, the way you look, your roles, and your daily routines. Things that you may have done with ease throughout your life may no longer be possible or may be done only with difficulty. Your hair may be thinning, and your skin, pale. You may have gone from taking care of others to having others take care of you. And daily routines may now consist of less time working and more time resting.

Adjusting to and accepting myriad changes are tough for most people. In the process of coming to terms with the inevitable changes, you may tend to focus on what's wrong with you and what you can't do. However, that does not serve you well. A more helpful approach is to pay attention to and sincerely consider what *is* right with you and what you *can* do. Some examples: You may have lost your hair or youthful figure, but your eyes still sparkle. You may not be able to meet the physical needs of your family, but you can still listen and share sound advice. You may not be able to go to work at the office, but you can still manage your personal affairs. You may not be able to hike up a rugged mountain, but you can walk your dog. Despite the changes in health, functioning, roles, and routines, the essence of who you are doesn't change; you are still you. And, as I've often heard founder of the mindfulness-based stress reduction program Jon Kabat-Zinn say, as long as you are here, "There is more right with you than wrong."

71

Accepting Changes—*What Is Right with Me*

Write about what is right with you at this moment in time: What are you capable of doing and experiencing? What parts of your body still work, and how do you make a difference in others' lives?

Each Day...

- Choose one personal-care activity (such as brushing your teeth, brushing your hair, taking a shower or a bath, shaving, putting on lotion, or taking medication) and do it mindfully. Do so with a quality of attention and care that conveys that you want to do it and that you deserve to be cared for so well.

- Choose one household activity (like making the bed, washing the dishes, or sweeping the floor) and do it mindfully. Be aware of the satisfaction you feel from bringing awareness to the experience.

- When you walk upstairs, pay attention to walking up the stairs. When you walk downstairs, pay attention to walking down the stairs.

Keep in Mind

There are countless opportunities to practice mindfulness in the course of a regular day during routine activities, like eating, walking, doing household chores, or brushing your teeth. While you may be aware of the changes in your body and your ability to do everyday activities, recognize what is right with you and what you are still capable of doing.

PART 2

~

COMPASSION

6

❧

OPENING THE DOOR: COMPASSION, KINDNESS, AND FORGIVENESS

If you maintain a feeling of compassion, of loving-kindness, then something automatically opens your inner door.
— The Dalai Lama XIV, *The Art of Happiness*

Life can sometimes make you bitter, defensive, or dulled. Cumulative hardships and broken dreams can create a metaphorical iron shell around your heart. As a result, you may have lost touch with your innate goodness—the seeds of kindness that were planted in you as a child—which is still with you yet just needs to be tended and nourished. No matter how old you are or how hardened your heart has become, you can always revive the lovely flower within you. And in doing so, you open the door to healing within and you create warmth and spaciousness that unites you with others and the world around you. Sharon Salzberg, a gifted meditation teacher, says, "When we can recover knowledge of our own loveliness and that of others, self-blessing happens naturally and beautifully" (Salzberg 2004, 22).

Looking back in history, we can see that the most remarkable people of the world have been those who have selflessly offered themselves in the spirit of alleviating others' suffering. Jesus Christ, Mahatma Gandhi, Mother Teresa, Nelson Mandela, and the Dalai Lama are just a few of the many great people whose kindheartedness blossomed amid their own anguish in witnessing the suffering of others. Their compassion was unconditional. It bubbled like a fountain within them and flowed to those who inflicted harm. More recently, we can observe this quality in Aung San Suu Kyi, a pro-democracy leader from Burma who was under house arrest for fifteen years. After years of restraint, she's not bitter, and her light of kindness hasn't dimmed; she is still an endless source of encouragement and compassion. In a *Time* magazine interview published less than two months after the house arrest was lifted (Beech/Rangoon 2010), she stated, "In my life, I have been showered with kindness. More than love, I value kindness. Love comes and goes, but kindness remains."

Compassion

A friend of mine, Sarah, told me a story that illustrates how you can act with true compassion in everyday life. Her mother-in-law is a challenging person, for not just Sarah but also most others. If things don't go her way, her mother-in-law goes off on a tirade, screaming and belittling others. Her mother-in-law's selfish and hurtful ways not only push everyone away but also make others dislike her intensely. During a recent outburst, Sarah noted an unanticipated shift in how she viewed her mother-in-law. She saw her as a fragile and insecure child who needed to be cuddled by her mother. At that moment, Sarah softened and opened to her mother-in-law with deep sincerity. Rather than retreat or defensively lash out, Sarah responded, "I know this must be hard for you. If I have contributed in any way to your difficulties now, I am sorry." For the first time in what seemed to be hours of chaos, there was stillness, like a pregnant pause. Her mother-in-law looked at Sarah, and their eyes connected. Her mother-in-law's face softened, and Sarah walked over and hugged her. Sarah's embrace was not merely a case of going through the motions, but from genuine tenderness and a heartfelt desire to alleviate her mother-in-law's suffering.

Compassion goes beyond being nice to people and wishing for them to be happy. Compassion is a heartfelt wish to relieve others' suffering. It is a felt experience within the body, sparked by unselfish and altruistic concern. Compassion involves relating to another's emotional or physical pain, or both, *and* having the motivation to assuage the pain.

While compassion is certainly other focused, it's important to recognize the value of self-compassion. Compassion toward yourself provides the foundation to be compassionate toward others. Self-compassion means to look within and engender a feeling of warm caring and true aspiration for relief of your own suffering. Having self-compassion doesn't mean that you are selfish. Being kind to yourself and taking away your own anguish opens the door for you to be receptive, kind, and helpful to others. Some people with serious illness are hard on themselves. They blame themselves for having the disease and feel guilty that they have become a burden to their loved ones. Cultivation of self-compassion and forgiveness is vital to melt the frigid remorse that limits healing and connectedness.

Research on Compassion Practices

There's a growing body of research that demonstrates the unquestionable beneficial effects of being compassionate and how this human quality can be cultivated. Progress in this area has been made thanks to the vision and efforts of the Mind & Life Institute, a nonprofit organization dedicated to building a scientific understanding of the mind, with the goals of reducing individual and societal suffering and promoting well-being. Significant research on compassion (and mindfulness) is being done at several prestigious institutions and programs, such as the University of Wisconsin Center for Investigating Healthy Minds and the Emory Collaborative for Contemplative Studies at Emory University.

Richie Davidson, Antoine Lutz, and their colleagues at the University of Wisconsin have conducted a number of experiments on compassion meditation. Much of what they've learned is through comparisons of adept compassion practitioners (specifically, Buddhist monks who have practiced compassion meditation for literally tens of thousands of hours) to novices (essentially, ordinary people without any experience in learning formal practices to cultivate compassion). They have demonstrated that compassion practices relate to activation of brain regions involved with emotion, empathy, and planning body movement in response to evocative sounds, like distressing screams or cries (Lutz, Brefczynski-Lewis, et al. 2008). These findings imply that cultivating compassion enhances a person's emotional feelings, sense of shared experience with another, and readiness to act and take away suffering. Additionally, these investigators have shown a link between compassion practices and high-frequency brain activity, called *gamma waves* (Lutz et al. 2004). Experienced compassion meditators have a strikingly greater magnitude of gamma waves compared to novices. Gamma waves represent integration of physically and functionally distinct regions of the brain. In essence, the brain is in synchrony, and its various regions work together as an efficient whole.

Colleagues at Emory University, Charles Raison, Lobsang Negi, and Thad Pace, are embarking on promising work to teach compassion practices to people without any background in meditation and to evaluate effects on the body and the mood. They have found that college students who were taught compassion meditation over a period of six weeks were less emotionally distressed and had lower levels of an inflammatory chemical substance in the body, called *interleukin-6*, than students not taught compassion practices. Specifically, they found that the students who benefited most were those who meditated more (did the most homework) (Pace et al. 2009).

Other research has explored the personal attribute of being self-compassionate in relation to dealing with unpleasant life events (Leary et al. 2007). In this work, self-compassion was shown to buffer against negative self-feelings. People who are self-compassionate acknowledge their roles in adverse events, yet they aren't reactive and overwhelmed with negative emotions, such as anger, guilt, anxiety, and sadness.

Loving-Kindness

Loving-kindness is unconditional goodwill. It is the aspiration for everyone to be happy and well, whether or not they are suffering. It is like a deep well of kindheartedness and wholesome deeds that are freely shared, not restricted only to those who are clearly in need, or those whom you like.

You can cultivate loving-kindness through meditation practices that date back nearly two thousand years. These practices are reflections or sincere wishes for goodness for all: yourself, those you hold dear and in high regard, acquaintances, those with whom you have difficulty, and all people and beings.

When we cultivate loving-kindness, we naturally feel better and subsequently are more connected with others and want to assist them. Barbara Fredrickson, a social psychologist at the University of North Carolina in Chapel Hill and leader in the field of positive psychology, has developed and tested the *broaden-and-build theory* of positive emotions. This work posits that experiences of positive emotions (such as joy, interest, pride, contentment, and love) broaden the way we think and respond to different circumstances, which in turn helps to build enduring resources within us that make us more resilient in undesirable circumstances (Fredrickson 2001). She and her colleagues have discovered that learning and practicing loving-kindness meditation over several weeks indeed increases positive emotions, like happiness and peace of mind, and lessens lingering negative emotions, like anger and sadness. Additionally, they found that loving-kindness practice fosters greater meaning in life, promotes feeling more supported by family and friends, and decreases illness-related symptoms, like pain (Fredrickson et al. 2008). In related work, James Carson and colleagues at Duke University School of Medicine in North Carolina demonstrated that an eight-week loving-kindness meditation program reduces anger and lessens pain in people with chronic back pain. This study elucidates the connection between challenging emotions (anger in this case) and physical symptoms (such as back pain) and how a practice of opening up your heart (through loving-kindness meditation) can dissolve destructive emotions and alleviate persistent symptoms, thus enhancing well-being (Carson et al. 2005). Furthermore, another study demonstrated that after just a short time (within minutes) of learning and practicing a brief loving-kindness exercise, people felt more positive about and connected to others. These findings indicate that the practice of loving-kindness can decrease your sense of social isolation (Hutcherson, Seppala, and Gross 2008).

～ MEDITATION PRACTICE ～
Loving-Kindness

The following guided meditation practice is directed toward the cultivation of goodwill, or loving-kindness, to a special loved one and yourself. Note, though, that this practice can also be extended to others: someone else for whom you have high regard (like a dear friend or revered teacher), someone whom you feel neutral toward (like an acquaintance), someone whom you feel particularly challenged by, or, more broadly, all people and beings.

- Bring to mind a loved one or someone who has been kind to you.

  - Smile as you bring this person to mind. If you'd like, you can rest your hand on your chest, over your heart, as you do this practice.

  - Visualizing this person and perhaps saying the person's name, sincerely wish her goodness, using the following phrases or other words that feel more right for you. Slowly read each phrase and allow the words to resonate, so you can feel them in your heart.

    May you be free from harm.
    May you be free from worry, fear, and anger.
    May you be happy.
    May you be physically healthy and strong.
    May you accept things as they are.
    May you live with ease.

- With the same degree of sincerity and kind regard, address yourself as you just addressed someone you cherish.

  - Smile gently and place your hand over your heart, if you'd like.

  - Allow this deep aspiration to fill you, using the following phrases or other words that may feel more right for you. Slowly read each phrase and allow the words to resonate, so you can feel them in your heart.

    May I be free from harm.
    May I be free from worry, fear, and anger.
    May I be happy.
    May I be free from pain.
    May I accept things as they are.
    May I be at ease, moment by moment.

Forgiveness

At sixty years old, Tony continues to be plagued by a traumatic divorce that happened over twenty-five years ago. Every day since its occurrence, he replays in his mind his ex-wife's hurtful words and devastating actions. He sees her as having destroyed his life by taking away his children, placing a restraining order on him, and securing huge alimony payments, leaving him with nothing. What she did was so spiteful and egregious that he would never consider forgiving her. Even now, as he lives with metastatic prostate cancer, he is troubled by his ex-wife's deceit and feels its corrosive aftermath day after day, year after year.

Like Tony, some people harbor grudges for decades. They resent the fact that they were harmed by another and simply can't let go of this part of the past. On the other hand, others hold on to feelings of remorse for having hurt or betrayed someone else.

PAUSE NOW: Consider for a moment: Have you felt bitter toward someone who has done you wrong? Or, are you unforgiving of yourself for having hurt another?

81

Harboring Grudges

Being resentful and unforgiving (toward yourself or another) can take its toll on your mental and physical health. It creates inner turmoil and tension that festers and leads to stress in the body, which can subsequently have a deleterious effect on your health (vanOyen Witvliet, Ludwig, and Vander Laan 2001). Research has shown that harboring grudges for years is associated with significant health problems, like increased risk of heart attack, high blood pressure, stomach ulcers, and pain disorders (such as arthritis, back problems, headaches, and chronic pain). People who bear grudges also are more likely to smoke, which is an unhealthy behavior that puts a person at risk for a number of other health problems (Messias et al. 2010).

Forgiveness Is the Antidote

Forgiveness is the antidote for resentment, bitterness, and regret. It involves having mercy on others who may have hurt you and self-mercy for having hurt others or yourself. Everett Worthington and colleagues, in an article that extensively discusses theories and research about forgiveness, note that it's possible to overcome unforgiveness (being begrudging, resentful, hateful, angry, and bitter) and to emotionally forgive (in your mind without necessarily going through the act of forgiving someone face to face) by experiencing positive emotions toward others, such as compassion, empathy, sympathy, love, and gratitude (Worthington et al. 2005). Therefore, many of the practices described throughout this book can facilitate your readiness and ability to forgive others and yourself for harm done in the past.

⟿ MEDITATION PRACTICE ⟿
Making Room for Forgiveness

- Allow yourself to settle into a comfortable position, and for a few moments, bring awareness to the sensations of the rise and fall of your abdomen with each inbreath and outbreath. Notice how you feel right now.

- If you'd like, you may place your hand over your heart as you do this practice.

- Silently repeat the following phrase a few times. Allow the words to resonate, so you can feel them in your heart.

  May I know forgiveness.

- Now consider instances when you may have hurt others, knowingly or unknowingly.

- Use the following phrases or other words that may feel more right for you. With each phrase, allow the words to resonate, so you can feel them in your heart.

  May I forgive myself.
  May I forgive myself for any pain I caused others and myself.
  May I forgive myself for mistakes made.
  May I forgive myself for things left undone.

- Notice if you have resistance to forgiving yourself. Breathe into the resistance.

- Now consider an instance or instances when others have done you wrong.

- To the degree that you are ready at this moment, extend your forgiveness.

- Use the following phrases or other words that feel more right for you. With each phrase, allow the words to resonate, so you can feel them in your heart.

  I forgive you.
  I forgive you for hurt or harm done to me.
  May I freely forgive all those who have hurt or harmed me, knowingly or unknowingly.

- Notice if you have resistance to forgiving others. Breathe into the resistance.

- Notice how you feel right now.

Each Day...

Silently send good wishes to another person. This may be someone who is going through a hard time or someone who isn't. It may be a loved one, an acquaintance, or someone who especially challenges you.

Keep in Mind

Compassion, kindness, and forgiveness can open your inner door to healing and create warmth and spaciousness that unites you with others and the world around you.

7

~

EXPANDING GENEROSITY AND SHARING IN OTHERS' DELIGHT

A kind heart is a fountain of gladness, making everything in its vicinity freshen into its smiles.

—Washington Irving

I recall a conversation that I had with a dear and wise elderly friend named Leo. Leo was a successful entrepreneur with a lovely, generous spirit. Over the years, he had unselfishly given his money and time to help individuals and community organizations. One day we were sitting in his living room surrounded by antiques and prized artwork, and he said, "Look around. All of this can't help me when I get sicker, and it won't prevent me from dying. And I can't take any of it with me. That's why I want to give and share with others in need as long as I am here and am able. And, you know, this makes me feel really good."

Leo's sensible and inspiring advice has stuck with me for many years. Indeed, giving makes us feel good. Research supports this: people who are altruistic are happier than those who aren't, and the benefits of selfless giving far outweigh the benefits of receiving (Schwartz et al. 2003). However, many people in our modern world are guided by the conviction that more money and material wealth will make them happier. The truth is that once our basic needs are met and we can live comfortably, more doesn't necessarily equal better. This is reflected in the well-known fact that people in the most affluent countries are actually, in general, the most disenfranchised. Look around a typical city in the United States, and you see people busily running around, gluttonously accumulating possessions and looking forward to the day they can retire. Despite a person's best planning, sometimes retirement never comes. Tragedy and serious illness can strike at any time, often when we least expect it. So, after years of accruing possessions and saving money, remember that none of it can go with you when you leave this world. By nurturing a spirit of generosity *now*, you will likely reap boundless benefits. You will feel joyful and liberated, and you will be fulfilled in realizing the difference you make to others. Your desire to give can go beyond possessions and money. Giving of yourself, in more personal and less tangible ways, such as sharing stories of your life, your favorite recipes, or art you've created, for example, is tremendously meaningful and will likely have an indelible effect on others.

Like generosity, empathetic joy is a wholesome quality that unites us with others and makes us feel good. "Empathetic joy" is composed of two words: "empathy" and "joy." Empathy is the ability to share another's feelings. European neuroscientist Tania Singer and her colleagues are elucidating what happens in the body when a person is empathetic. In one study, they found that areas of the brain associated with being in pain are activated simply by watching a loved one who is exposed to a painful probe (Singer et al. 2004). Essentially, seeing someone you love suffer can trigger a similar effect in your body, as if it were actually happening to you. Joy is a positive emotion associated with delight and feeling good. Thus, empathetic joy is feeling genuine contentment when you recognize that another is joyful: you're happy when you see that others are happy. Rather than harbor jealousy or envy when someone else has good health or good luck, try opening your heart and letting gladness fill you, without expecting anything in return. It's likely that you will feel better, because there will be a wonderful ripple effect and the joy will multiply exponentially.

Meaningful Giving

In recognizing that this is the last phase of your life, have you thoughtfully decided what, how, and when you would give to others? How can your giving be most meaningful to you and to those you care about? Have you distributed all of your belongings, even those of high sentimental yet low monetary value, to those who would cherish them most? Are there personal and less tangible ways that you can share a part of you that will leave enduring positive memories for your family and future generations? When is the best time to give—is it face to face, while you are alive, or would you rather leave instructions to be followed after you've gone? These are questions worth exploring. By reflecting on and working through them now, you will have greater peace of mind, and in the process you may also feel closer to your loved ones. If you prefer to not give away anything while you are alive, at least sort it out and make plans accordingly. It's best to put your wishes in writing, in a will or a letter, to avoid potential confusion down the road.

Letting Go of Material Belongings

Look around you. Everything you own will end up somewhere: your family's home, a local charity's secondhand store, an auction house, or in the trash. Nothing you own will go with you when you die. Therefore, you can leave it up to others to determine, or you can play an active role and decide the fate of your souvenirs, mementos, and other special possessions or things you've worked hard to acquire. The choice is yours.

Giving away your possessions in person, while you are alive, could be extremely rewarding for you and the recipients. Consider giving your children or grandchildren something of great sentimental value to you and telling them a story about it. Watching a person's face light up will surely elate your spirit, too.

PAUSE NOW: Take a moment to notice how you feel right now as you consider your belongings and their fate.

Personal Touch: Sharing a Part of You

There are literally countless ways that you can share a part of you with the special people in your life—heartfelt extensions of you, on which you cannot put a price tag. People will be deeply touched and fondly remember you through this kind of thoughtful giving. Some examples are sharing stories about your life (perhaps recorded with a digital audio or video recorder, so others can remember the details and continue to hear your voice and see you); documenting your family tree; writing letters or poems; composing songs; creating artwork or handiwork; and sharing family recipes and photographs. Remember that whatever you give is uniquely you, so the possibilities are plentiful. Also consider leaving something meaningful for those members of your family who are yet to be born. This could be a way that they can know you, even though they won't have a chance to meet you.

My mother was an avid and talented knitter. Even when her health declined in the last years of her life, Mom continued to knit. She made many beautiful sweaters, afghans, socks, and baby outfits and gave them to everyone in the family. To this day, nearly thirty years later, I still cherish the knitted goodies that Mom made, and I think of her and smile whenever I wear them. And the baby outfits she made have been passed down to all of my nephews, most of who were born after she had passed away.

In research that I codirected with esteemed music therapist Suzanne Hanser, women with advanced breast cancer participated in a program using music to help them cope with the challenges they were facing (Hanser et al. 2006). One participant shared the following:

> I wrote a song [with the music therapist] for my grandchildren, who haven't been born yet. It was very cathartic. It makes me feel so much better to know that I have written down basically everything I would ever want to say to them, even though I will probably not be around when they are born. It was a wonderful experience.

I also recall Dennis, a man in his fifties whom I worked with when I was a hospice nurse. Dennis wrote a letter for every special person in his life, including each of his children and grandchildren (including those yet to be born). Each letter was personalized and described the qualities he admired in the person, special memories of shared experiences, and his hopes and dreams for the person's future.

～ REFLECTIVE PRACTICE ～
Caring by Sharing

- Allow yourself to settle, bringing awareness to the experience of breathing or to other bodily sensations. Do this for a minute or two, with your eyes closed or gazing softly in front of you. Notice how you feel.

- Consider the significant people in your life.

- For each person, consider if there is anything you would like to give, either something you've owned or a part of you.

  - What is it?
  - What would be the most meaningful way to share it with that person?
  - How can you increase the likelihood that you will be able to give it to the person in the manner that you'd like?

- After you've contemplated the previous queries for each of the significant people in your life, tune in and notice how you feel right now. Allow yourself to feel whatever is arising in you. Stay with it and breathe into it without trying to change anything.

Sharing in Others' Delight

Consider people you may know who seem to have an easy life. They may be bestowed with good health, talents, loving relationships, financial security, and, perhaps from your perspective, not a care in the world. How do you feel when you bring these people to mind?

In general, it's easier to rejoice in others' good fortunes when you feel well and happy yourself, or when you like the person. The challenge is how to experience shared gladness regardless of circumstances: when you don't feel well, when you don't like the person, and when there is *nothing in it* for you (meaning you don't get anything as a result of the other person's good luck).

You may wonder why you ought to unconditionally share in another's happiness. The alternative is to feel envious or to be indifferent. Envy is a destructive emotion that can fog your ability to see things as they are, including any goodness that may be before you. It can restrict you, wear you down, and make you irritable. While being indifferent is certainly less caustic than envying someone, it has qualities of dullness and apathy that inhibit you from experiencing vividness and pleasure and seeing basic goodness in others. So consider what might happen if you were to open up and share delight in another's good health, joy, and good fortune.

~ MEDITATION PRACTICE ~
Empathetic Joy

- Bring to mind someone for whom you have high regard who is happy and has goodness in his life, such as good health, talents, prosperity, a loving family, a comfortable home, or an overall good life. It can be just one of these attributes, since realistically no one has a perfect life. This person can be a loved one, a friend, or a dear teacher.

  - Smile as you bring this person to mind.
  - From the bottom of your heart, allow gladness to fill you.
  - Wish for this person:

    May you continue to be happy.
    May your good fortune not leave you.
    May the goodness in your life flourish.

- Now bring to mind someone whom you feel neutral toward who is happy and has apparent goodness in her life. You know this person but don't have a personal relationship with her, and no instant feeling of like or dislike comes up as you imagine her.

  - Smile as you bring this person to mind.
  - From the bottom of your heart, allow gladness to fill you.
  - Wish for this person:

    May you continue to be happy.
    May your good fortune not leave you.
    May the goodness in your life flourish.

- Now bring to mind someone whom you dislike, who dislikes you, or who has been challenging for you and is happy and has apparent goodness in his life.

  - Smile as you bring this person to mind.
  - From the bottom of your heart, allow gladness to fill you.
  - Wish for this person:

    May you continue to be happy.
    May your good fortune not leave you.
    May the goodness in your life flourish.

  - Notice if you feel resistance. If so, breathe into the resistance.

- Bring awareness to how you feel right now.

Each Day...

Give to others, even in seemingly small and intangible ways, like extending a compliment. Smile when you see others who are graced with good health and good luck.

Keep in Mind

By nurturing a spirit of generosity, you will likely be fulfilled as you see the difference you make to others. Opening up your heart and rejoicing in others' delight can help to dissolve envy and can promote a feeling of well-being within yourself.

8

APPRECIATING NOW AND THEN

There is a calmness to a life lived in gratitude, a quiet joy.
—Ralph H. Blum

Life changes when you have a life-limiting illness. Things that brought you great pleasure in the past may be less a part of your world now. For example, your ability to travel, attend events, dance, exercise, cook, or do projects may be restricted. While you may not be able to do what you used to do, this is an opportunity for you to learn about yourself in a new way. It is an opportunity to savor goodness in your life right now, in ways that may surprise you, and to reflect on earlier life experiences in such a way that you feel gratitude and enrichment in who you are in the present moment.

We are all familiar with the proverb "Count your blessings." Though the cliché may be overused, the message remains profound. Most people don't actually take the time to *deeply* reflect on the blessings bestowed on them. Those who face a serious illness may be inspired to take inventory of life's gifts as a way of creating meaning and putting their lives in perspective. Some, though, find it difficult to tap into a sense of gratitude because they feel victimized or are filled with anger or sadness about what is happening to them.

Benefits of Being Grateful

Being grateful is actually good for us. Intuitively we know this, and research supports this notion. Studies led by Robert Emmons from the University of California–Davis and Michael McCullough from the University of Miami have documented the personal benefits of gratitude (also referred to as gratefulness, appreciation, and thankfulness). People who are thankful for what they have in their lives are happier, less sad and depressed, more satisfied with life in general, more energized and optimistic, and less stressed than those who do not have a grateful attitude (Emmons and McCullough 2003; McCullough, Emmons, and Tsang 2002). It is not as if they see the world through rose-colored glasses, since studies show that grateful people don't deny the negative aspects of life. They are able to integrate both good and bad in ways that bring meaning and appreciation, while placing little value on material possessions. In the ups and downs of life, simple nonmaterial things matter most. Grateful people also have a keen awareness of being connected to others. They are kindhearted and genuinely care about the welfare of others. They abundantly share what they have and reach out to those in need. As a result of feeling blessed and fulfilled, they naturally overflow with compassion and generosity.

Not everyone, though, has a grateful disposition. The good news is that people can cultivate this quality through reflection and writing. Research studies have shown the value of keeping a gratitude journal. People who write down and track aspects of their lives for which they are thankful feel better physically (have fewer symptoms) and mentally (are happier and more optimistic), and they are more likely to attain personal life goals than those who write about other things, such as daily hassles and life events, or how they are better off than others (Emmons and McCullough 2003). After maintaining a written log of small and big things for which they were grateful, people with debilitating neuromuscular disease experienced greater joy, vitality, and connectedness to others. They also slept more soundly and had a greater overall positive outlook on life (ibid.). In summary, the research shows that being grateful—whether it is from having a natural disposition or developing it through practices like writing—enhances well-being and strengthens the quality of interpersonal connections in those with and without serious illness alike. The bottom line is that being grateful is good for you, in more ways than one.

Gratefulness and Living Fully

Brother David Steindl-Rast has written and spoken extensively on the virtues of gratefulness. To him, gratefulness is inherent in living fully, and it is not possible to live a full life if we do not recognize the myriad gifts before us every day (Steindl-Rast 1984). As Brother David says, we must "wake up" (ibid., 7). We must have fresh and alert eyes to notice the surprises that reveal themselves when we are awake enough to see them, and allow them to fill us with a sense of awe. In those moments of recognition and wonderment, we can embrace an inner knowing of being grateful. Gratefulness is the entry to opening our hearts with compassion: to look into the eyes of others with softness and kindness, recognize and appreciate what they have done for you, and genuinely wish them abundant goodness.

Taking Stock in Simple Pleasures

The cultivation of mindfulness is the key to waking up and fully experiencing simple pleasures. Simple pleasures are small things that don't cost much, if anything at all. They include going to bed with fresh, clean sheets; taking a bubble bath; listening to a string quartet; looking up at the moon and stars; licking a strawberry ice cream cone; sipping on a cup of tea in front of a crackling fire; and watching children at the playground. The list of possible simple pleasures is limitless and varies from one person to another. What one person experiences as pleasurable, another may not. You may even find that your simple pleasures may change from day to day depending on how you feel, the weather, whom you are with, or whatever may arise unexpectedly. It is important that you pay attention to the small treasures that await you. If you're completely preoccupied with your doctor's appointment next week, you might miss the rare migratory birds outside your window right now. For each simple pleasure that you are blessed to be aware of and experience, pause, smile, and be grateful for that moment, a moment of unfiltered goodness.

During the last two years of my father's life, he lost his ability to swallow. The simple pleasures associated with eating and drinking that most of us take for granted were stripped from this man of few words. In his retirement my dad had delighted in daily trips to the market for fresh vegetables, seafood or meat, and mindfully mastering a gustatory creation that he then savored while sipping on a glass of Merlot. Going out to eat, one of his great pastimes, and planning and preparing holiday meals for family and friends were no longer options. Even swallowing a spoonful of ice cream, a single ice chip, or his own saliva was difficult and carried serious consequences (for example, infection in his lungs).

The road to finding and experiencing new pleasures was not easy for my father. Yet it was possible. His yellow Labrador retriever, Daisy, brought him immeasurable joy. His face would melt into a grin as he looked into Daisy's big, brown eyes as she laid her head on his chest whenever they rested together on the sofa. He would pat her belly, and she would express her gratitude by licking his face. Quiet time with Daisy mattered more than anything else to Dad. He silently thanked her every day for being his best friend and loyal companion.

Dad was also grateful that he could still walk and go for short strolls outside his home (a far cry from his days as a serious marathon runner). He would sit in a lawn chair with Daisy at his feet and soak in the New England sun. He was enlivened by birdsong; puffy clouds floating across the indigo sky; maple trees swaying in the breeze; and the fresh, crisp Vermont mountain air as it filled his lungs. Nature was nourishing. "Simple" was satisfying.

I am also reminded of a thirty-eight-year-old woman named Jennifer, who had an extended hospitalization for cancer treatment. She returned home with fresh eyes after weeks in the hospital. Home had been a familiar comfort, yet she was able to experience it in ways she had never experienced before. She shared the following:

The other day I was standing at the radiator, just ready to pick up something to read, and thought, Aah, I am at the radiator. It is warm. I am in my home. Isn't this lovely.

PAUSE NOW: Pause for a moment, expand your field of awareness, and answer these questions:

What simple pleasures are true for me right now?

What can I see, hear, smell, taste, or feel that is pleasing to me in this moment?

What pleasant colors, shades of light, shapes, scents, flavors, or skin sensations am I aware of?

Let gratitude fill you. Rest in the awareness of being grateful.

Appreciating Others' Love and Care

You can extend appreciation to others who have made a difference in your life from an early age and throughout the years up to the present time. From the moment of your birth and throughout your childhood years, you received love and care from elders who supported you and helped build a good foundation for the rest of your life. They may be parents, grandparents or other family members, or others who are not related to you, like neighbors, teachers, or counselors. Even if you came from a troubled home, someone has looked out for you and provided caring guidance as you've made your way in the world. As you've matured, your circle has likely expanded to include friends, a spouse, children, nieces and nephews, new neighbors, more teachers, and pets. Whether they are living or now deceased, each has helped to shape who you are with love, care, and counsel. Have you ever acknowledged and expressed gratitude to these people face to face, in letters, on the phone, or just silently to yourself?

When you consider your world as it is today, who are those special loved ones who provide the wind beneath your wings, a shoulder to lean on when you are falling over, a receptive ear when you need to vent, and that warm hug when you feel completely undone? Beyond their practical assistance in *doing* things for you—like driving you to appointments, helping to keep your business straight, making meals, doing laundry, cleaning the house, or shopping—are you aware of what it is like *being* with them? Do you notice how they convey their love and caring through the way they look, listen, touch, or simply be with you? What small and big ways are they there for you? Have you adequately expressed your gratitude to the special people in your life currently?

Now consider the health care professionals and care assistants who provide kind and compassionate care to you, perhaps day after day, year after year: your nurse, doctor, home health aide, social worker, massage therapist, physical therapist, or mental health counselor, among others. Sure, it may be their job to help care for you, but you can tell who the special ones are: those who are genuinely concerned about you and your well-being and who go above and beyond the basic call of duty.

Steve, a fifty-year-old insurance agent with cancer, said this about learning mindfulness and how it affected his perspective on the health care professionals who took care of him during an extended hospitalization:

> I think it gave me a heightened awareness of the level of care I was getting. It's a privilege. I mean I would rather not be in the situation at all, but since I am, it's wonderful to be treated so well.

PAUSE NOW: Pause for a moment and consider your care providers. What is the quality of their presence? How are they there for you? How do you feel as you bring them to mind? Have you adequately expressed your gratitude to these special care providers?

Looking Back

The value of looking back and reflecting on your life has been well recognized and found to be particularly helpful in managing depression in older people (Bohlmeijer, Smit, and Cuijpers 2003). You can expand this process of looking back by engendering a feeling of gratefulness as you consider the life you have lived. In doing so, you may find that it helps you to make sense of and find meaning in your life as a whole, gain perspective, and appreciate the different aspects of the life you've lived—the pinnacles, the pitfalls, and the special people—and how you've grown as a person.

After a severe stroke, Troy, a seventy-year-old retired engineer, is living with progressive heart failure and complications from a stroke. He has considerable difficulty walking, talking, and eating. Despite the gross losses he has experienced, Troy treasures what he still has, namely, his mind. As an engineer, his mind served him well, and though he is ill, Troy can still analyze, solve equations, and remember. His intact memory remains keen as he spends many hours reflecting on his life, a life well lived. He recalls his modest beginnings as a child and skipping stones with his best friend, the fortuitous meeting that landed him a scholarship to Massachusetts Institute of Technology (MIT), the mentoring he received from a famous professor, college memories, meeting his wife, and the special gatherings with his children and grandchildren. He also considers the challenging memories, like his lost job, his stillborn child, and his current illness. As the different images of the past play in his mind, Troy is filled with gratitude for the rich experiences that have given him meaning and strength. In his mind's eye, Troy can bring vividness of past experiences to the present moment in such a way that he is filled with vitality and joy right now. Gratitude fills every cell of his body as he acknowledges the abundant gifts that have showered his life for the last seven decades.

Obstacles to Feeling Grateful

You may find it hard to be receptive and to feel grateful, especially when you are feeling angry, irritable, crabby, or in pain. Rather than beat yourself up because you can't feel thankful, acknowledge it and sit with it. Observe your thoughts and feelings, notice how they shift, and be receptive to gaining insight into what you are thinking and how you are feeling. Be gentle with yourself and recognize that you cannot force yourself to feel grateful. Allow it to naturally emerge in a way that feels authentic. It will reveal itself through the cultivation of mindfulness and compassion. The practices explored in this book can help create a fertile ground for gratefulness to surface and grow.

~ REFLECTIONS ON GRATEFULNESS ~

You can do the following practices as meditations only or with the addition of writing in a journal. The goal here is to connect with aspects of your life, current and past, for which you are genuinely grateful.

- Allow your body to settle into a comfortable position and your mind to gently settle into the rhythm of your breathing or some other point of neutral awareness that may be more comfortable to you.

- Sit quietly and allow relevant images or experiences to emerge in your mind's eye. Let them resonate deeply. It is best to not rush this practice. For each aspect of your life for which you are grateful, spend at least five minutes reflecting and resting in awareness.

- Try to be specific and concrete in identifying and imagining each one.

  - *Right now in my life, I am grateful for:*

    The simple pleasures of nature, music, colors and light, children, scents, tastes, sensations, hobbies

    Special people who love and care about me

    Caring and competent professionals who take excellent care of me

    My pet

    The roof over my head

    My ability to...

- *As I look back on my past, I am grateful for:*

  Special people, alive or deceased, who have loved and cared about me: parents or grandparents; siblings; children; other relatives, such as aunts, uncles, and cousins; friends; teachers; former partners or lovers

  Meaningful or enjoyable work, or both

  Places I have visited

  Difficult experiences that have made me a stronger or better person

- Rest quietly and allow gratefulness to fill you. Notice how your body feels. Notice your thoughts and emotions as they arise.

- Notice if you have resistance to doing this practice. If so, where do you notice it? What does it feel like? Do not judge the resistance. Allow yourself to just be with it.

- Allow the gratefulness images and memories to naturally emerge. Try not to force them. If you are having a hard time visualizing images or experiences, or accessing memories, just be open to whatever arises in the quiet and spacious landscape of your mind.

- Try not to focus on the abstract idea of something, but rather bring to mind images of actual experiences with vivid details.

- You may choose to reflect on one or two of the previous list items in one sitting, or you may spread out the entire practice over several days.

- After you've gone through the list once, you can go back and repeat each one or just those that speak most to you. Allow new ideas, images, and memories to emerge. Again, allow yourself to fill with gratefulness and to feel it in your body.

Each Day...

- Take a few minutes to reflect on the goodness in your life right now.

- Say to yourself (or write down, or do both), *Today I am grateful for...*

- Be aware of simple pleasures, especially those you may not have noticed before.

Keep in Mind

Engendering a sense of gratefulness enhances your well-being and helps you to live more fully. You can be grateful for the goodness in your life right now, such as simple pleasures and love and care from others. And you can also look back and be grateful for aspects of the life you've lived. Being angry and irritated can interfere with feeling grateful, but you can overcome those obstacles by using regular practices that help you to settle your mind and open your heart.

PART 3

CONNECTEDNESS

9

~

ACCEPTING HELP

Asking for help is an affirmation that you believe in yourself, you recognize an answer is available, and you are open to receive it.

—Alan Cohen

Accepting help from others is one of the greatest challenges for people with a serious illness. Basic everyday activities that you have done for yourself for as long as you can remember, like driving, cooking, and taking a shower, may now be difficult and necessitate assistance from family, friends, and professionals. This is especially difficult for people who have an independent spirit or for those who enjoy taking care of others. Furthermore, our society values a do-it-yourself attitude. Therefore, we have a natural tendency to resist help as long as possible or to deny that we ever need it. Accepting help may seem like a sign of weakness, dependence, or giving in to the illness. However, accepting help is actually a wise and essential step toward caring for yourself and an entry to opening up to love and care from others.

Sandra, a sixty-three-year-old retired nurse, mother, and grandmother, has prided herself on maintaining independence throughout her life. A natural caregiver, she is happiest when she is lending a hand and taking care of others. She has maintained an active lifestyle even after being diagnosed with metastatic breast cancer five years ago. Over the last few months,

Sandra has become more limited in what she can do. She has slowed down as a result of increasing pain, fatigue, and a general sense of feeling unwell.

Sandra has a strong network of friends and family, including her children and grandchildren, who live close by. They all adore her and would like to help her out. Despite their frequent offers to assist with shopping, cooking, cleaning and laundry, driving to appointments, and picking up prescriptions, and even though she feels wiped out, Sandra has been steadfast in her refusal of everyone's offers to help her. Sandra won't consider it; she stubbornly prefers to do it all herself. She is acutely aware, though, that she is having more and more difficulty getting by and managing everything that needs to get done. Moreover, she pushes others away and overexerts herself, only to find that she ends up feeling worse: the pain becomes unbearable, requiring more pain medication, and her energy level is zapped for days.

Deep down Sandra knows that she needs help, yet she won't ask for it or accept offers from others. Her fears, resistance, and unease with being on the other side of caregiving—as the care recipient—hold her back. She doesn't want to give in or give up. She is concerned that she will be viewed as weak and needy. Meanwhile those who care about Sandra stand quietly on the sidelines watching, feeling helpless and somewhat frustrated.

> **PAUSE NOW:** Take a moment to notice how you are feeling after reading Sandra's story. Simply pause and tune in. Be aware of what resonates with you in this example. Notice the bodily sensations and emotions that you are feeling right now. Consider how you actually respond to offers of assistance and if you ask for help when you need it.

From Resistance to Receptivity

While it's much more common than freely accepting and receiving help, resisting help is fraught with consequences. Trying to do everything yourself will likely leave you feeling depleted, perhaps with more aches, pains, and exhaustion. This then necessitates more rest, and you end up doing fewer of the things you like to do and having less quality time with your family and friends. Resisting assistance through your words or actions, like digging in your heels, is often infused with anger, sadness, and fear, and it poses a strain on your body, your relationships, and your spirit. Muscle tension, indigestion, shallow breathing, and rapid heart rate are some of the ways you may feel it in your body. Muscle tension, in particular, can contribute to already existing bone or muscle pain from the underlying disease. You may lash out or put up walls to keep out those people who are trying to help you. In turn you may feel bad and be self-deprecating for pushing them away. Resistance brings restriction. It causes mental and physical contraction, thereby limiting perspective, possibilities, and your ability to experience joy and love.

Receptivity, on the other hand, involves openness: open mind, body, and heart. By openly receiving others' help, there is a sense of acceptance of what is happening. There is softness and spaciousness in the experience of gracefully accepting and receiving assistance that translates into a lighter mood, a more relaxed body, connectedness with others, and a general ease in living. It also provides an opportunity for loved ones to demonstrate gratitude for the love and care you have provided to them over the years. It helps them to feel good about themselves and allows them to see that they can make a positive difference in your life. You see the satisfaction and fullness they experience when they help you. They feel help-*full* rather than help-*less*.

Receiving and accepting help doesn't mean that you need to lose your independence. You can have others help you *and* still do things yourself; they are not mutually exclusive. You and others can also do things together. The goal is for you to be aware of and discern what you can reasonably do yourself and what you actually need help with. Regular mindfulness practice helps with this discernment. Mindfulness facilitates seeing more clearly and making sound decisions as they relate to your self-care.

The postscript to Sandra's story is that she gradually opened up to receiving assistance from her family. She initiated this shift by asking her grown children to help with the laundry, and they gladly accepted. It was a team effort, because her son pulled together the dirty clothes and linens and put them in the washer; her daughter put them in the dryer; and they all folded, put away, and changed the linens. Accomplishing this together created an opportunity for them to share old stories and to laugh together. The positive experience with the laundry allowed Sandra to be receptive to allowing her children to help in other ways. She was gradually able to shift her view of what it meant to accept help, from losing independence to sharing quality time with those she cared about the most.

Breaking Down Barriers: Fear, Pride, and Habits

Three common barriers that interfere with receptivity to others' help are fear, pride, and habits. Fear may include fear of losing control, fear of giving up or giving in to the illness, and fear of being weak. Pride in this sense involves a rigid ego or sense of self that is attached to the notion of being independent. Here fear and pride often go hand in hand. While protective in the short run, they can create challenges in the long run. They inhibit you from being open to alternatives that might best meet your needs. Letting go of fear and pride, and honestly asking for and accepting help, actually puts you in control. You are in a position of strength, because you get to decide what you need and how others can best assist you. You may come to realize how your receptivity to others' caring and practical assistance has a positive effect not only on how you feel but also on how they feel. You may also realize how you're not alone and that you're really in this together.

Conditioned habits (such as reflexively not asking for help or saying no to offers of help) interfere with receptivity in accepting help. This is especially true for parents, who are conditioned to give help to rather than receive it from their children. Breaking old habits is possible, and you can learn this just as you learn any new skill. If you want to learn ballroom dancing, you can't walk onto the dance floor and be comfortable with all of the moves the first time. The key is to begin with small, deliberate steps with someone whom you trust. Little by little, small successes increase your confidence to make bigger and bolder steps until it becomes second nature. You then notice a difference in how you feel when you are open to others' help. You see that it can enhance rather than diminish your life, which makes it easier to do again.

They Said No When I Asked for Help

After you muster the confidence to ask for help, there may be times when someone responds by saying no or is unable to help you. You may feel crushed or outraged: *How can he say no when I really need him now?* When asking for help, it's best not to be attached to the outcome, meaning you can accept any way that it turns out. If others say no, it may reflect that they simply cannot be there for you in the way that you need them to be at this time. It doesn't necessarily mean that they will never be there for you, just that right now they are unable to be there for you. It may mean that they need to take care of their own needs before attending to yours, as with the direction the flight attendant gives you to put the oxygen mask on yourself before helping others. It may also mean that they are not capable of providing the particular assistance that you requested, but they may be glad to help in other ways. It's critical that you be honest with one another so that you can sincerely ask for help and so that your loved ones can gracefully decline. It is important to honor their responses, avoid being judgmental, and not take a refusal too personally. Return to an inner place of groundedness, clarity, and confidence. When the time feels right, try again to ask for help, with the same person or someone else.

There's No One to Ask for Help

You may live alone and feel isolated, as if you have no one to turn to for help. While you may not have the traditional support system of family and friends close by, consider thinking more creatively about your connections with others and who might be available for you if you reached out to them. Are there neighbors, old or new friends, or extended family with whom you have had a positive relationship? If you cannot identify anyone, you need to be open to professional assistance. Talking with your nurse, doctor, or social worker about the challenges you're having and how you have no one to help you is an important first step to getting the help you need.

Receiving and Accepting Help

- Settle your body and gently close your eyes or maintain a soft gaze. With kindness, settle your mind by bringing your attention to the sensations of breathing or to another neutral sensation that may be more comfortable for you. Simply rest in stillness and with awareness for a few moments.

- Think about a time when you needed something and didn't ask for help. Consider what prevented you from asking for assistance. What held you back? Be aware of how you feel right now as you bring this to mind.

- Bring to mind a time when you declined others' offers to help you but, deep down, knew you needed it. Who offered to help and what were the circumstances? What held you back from accepting the help? Do you feel unsettled or satisfied in how you handled this? Notice how you feel as you consider this.

- Bring to mind a time when you asked for help. Whom did you ask? What were the circumstances? How did the person respond to your request? How did you feel afterward? How do you feel right now as you consider this? If no situation in which you asked for help comes to mind, that's okay.

- Bring to mind someone whom you love and care about and who loves and cares about you. Imagine this person offering to assist you with something you need. Recognize the good intentions behind the offer. Sense how you feel as you gently open to this person's kindness and generosity. With a soft smile on your face, sincerely and gratefully accept this offer. Notice how you feel right now as you bring this image to mind.

- With this same person in mind, someone whom you love and care about and who loves and cares about you, imagine asking for help with something you need. Remember that this is someone whom you trust and who wants to help you. Allow yourself to open up to this person's caring. Ask the person for help in such a way that conveys your kindness and gratitude. Be aware of how you feel in this moment as you consider this.

∼ REFLECTIVE WRITING ∼
Opening Up to Others' Help

Write about a situation that you are currently having a hard time taking care of yourself, yet around which you have been unable to open up to ask for or receive others' help. Specifically write about what holds you back from asking for or accepting the help you need. Focus on your own issues that perpetuate resistance, such as your fears, your anger, your stubbornness, and your pride. Do not blame or belittle others; rather keep the focus on you and what you have the power to change, such as your attitude, your communication, and your actions. Make note of how you feel as you write this.

After you have written about what holds you back, write about ways you can gracefully receive others' assistance. Now notice how you feel right now—how your body feels and the emotions you are experiencing—and briefly note these sensations and feelings.

Each Day...

- Be mindful of when you engage in activities that you have to do, such as household chores, personal care (like bathing and getting dressed), and medical tasks (such as driving to appointments, getting prescriptions filled, organizing medications and treatments, submitting paperwork). Notice if you do them by yourself or if you involve others to help you out. Notice how you feel and whether you are pushing yourself too much or not.

- Look for new small ways to ask for help and notice how this experience feels.

- Catch yourself when you automatically resist or push away others when they offer to help you. When this happens, pause for a moment and mindfully take a deep breath. Try to soften into the experience and consider others' intentions in offering you help. Then make a conscious decision to openly accept or kindly decline their offers.

Keep in Mind

Openly accepting help may not be easy, but it has the potential to greatly enhance your quality of life as well as that of your loved ones. It involves listening to your body and being honest with yourself and others. Accepting help engenders a spirit of joining with those who deeply care about you. Mindfulness practices serve as a foundation to help you clearly see what you can reasonably do for yourself and also recognize when it is wise to ask for and accept assistance from others.

10

~

COMMUNICATING
MINDFULLY AND
WHOLEHEARTEDLY

Express yourself completely; then keep quiet.

—*Tao Te Ching*

Many people have a hard time speaking authentically, from the heart. In general, from an early age, we are conditioned to say what we think others may want to hear so that we will be liked, or we may close down and become reticent because of others' condemning reactions. However, communication grounded in truthfulness and mutual respect—when one person speaks clearly and honestly, and the other person listens with interest and sincerity—can be healing for you and for your relationship with the other person.

Communication during the last phase of your life can be especially challenging. There may be years of unspoken or misspoken words that have created barriers between you and others in your life. This is complicated by the time-sensitive importance of sharing your wishes, such as deciding to stop aggressive medical treatment and making funeral arrangements, and of expressing love, forgiveness, and thoughts you have wanted to share yet haven't. The proverb "If not now, then when?" comes to mind. If you don't purposefully make the effort to share what's on your mind and in your heart *now*, then you may lose the opportunity to ever do so.

The qualities of being calm and present, cultivated through the mindfulness practices described in part 1 of this book, serve as a foundation for you to be clear and genuine. The qualities of gentleness and respect, nurtured through the compassion practices explained in part 2 of this book, provide the basis for you to be kindhearted and empathetic. In essence, taken together, speaking and listening mindfully and wholeheartedly can foster inner healing and mutual understanding that may bring you closer to others despite past difficulties.

Difficult Conversations

Karen, a dear friend with metastatic malignant melanoma, knew her time was limited. She could sense her body changing and recognized that it was harder and harder for her to get around and take care of herself. Deep down, Karen knew that continuing with aggressive medical treatments would no longer help her. She was also tired of having the treatments, which caused her to spend most of her time at the clinic or in the hospital. She had already been poked and prodded for way too long, and she felt that enough was enough. She also described her desire to die at a lovely local residential hospice. I know this because we had many frank conversations; I was Karen's confidante, not part of her immediate family. While she shared how she felt with me, Karen also asked me to vow not to share this with her family. She indicated that her family wasn't ready and couldn't handle knowing how she felt, at least not yet. Karen didn't want to upset them, so she held back her feelings and passively continued with futile medical interventions. Her husband, Roger, clung to the belief that a miracle drug would come along and save her. Her mother, who rarely left her side, adored Karen, her only daughter, and encouraged her to keep eating and walking because it would make her stronger. Karen kept silent and dutifully followed what Roger and her mother wanted right up until her death in the intensive care unit.

In another case, a dear colleague of mine, who was a devoted husband, caring father, and great mentor to his students, was diagnosed with liver cancer. To cope with his illness and minimize disruptions to others, he tried to maintain normalcy. He was not particularly interested in discussing his prognosis and tried to keep up with his busy work schedule, including attending a faculty meeting just a few weeks before his death. On that fateful day, he passed away minutes before my hurried arrival. When I entered the bedroom, his wife was tightly embracing his body and wailing mournfully. Her bottled emotions and previously unspoken words poured out like effluence from a burst dam. She had never expressed her deep feelings and love while he was alive.

PAUSE NOW: Take a moment to notice how you feel after reading the previous stories. Simply pause and tune in. Be aware of what resonates with you in these examples. Notice the bodily sensations and emotions that you are feeling right now. Consider how you handle difficult conversations.

Common Reasons for Avoiding Difficult Conversations

Unfortunately, these stories are very common. I've witnessed countless others—people with incurable illness *and* their loved ones—who have held back from engaging in difficult conversations. Topics discussed in difficult conversations can be past issues, like healing old wounds; current issues, like sharing wishes related to medical care; future issues, like taking care of family and business matters; or conveying "I love you," "Thank you," and "Goodbye." There are three frequent reasons why people don't initiate these dialogues. First, some people have a hard time expressing their feelings and wishes candidly even under normal circumstances, let alone having those necessary-yet-difficult conversations as they approach or are in the last phase of life. Second, they don't want to upset others. Like Karen, the person who is sick may hold back in an effort to please others and be viewed as strong and not giving up. Family members also hold back as a way of protecting the loved one who is sick. Third, they superstitiously think that having such conversations, which either implicitly or explicitly acknowledge the gravity of the illness, would hasten death, as if not having such discussions would prevent it from happening. We know that this is not rational thinking, because no such cause-and-effect relationship has been shown to exist. On the contrary, one study showed that beginning palliative care early, an implicit acknowledgment that cure is not likely, resulted in longer survival, less depression, and better quality of life in people with advanced-stage lung cancer, compared to those who received conventional, aggressive medical care (Temel et al. 2010). Regardless of the reason, no one really benefits when the hard and honest talks are avoided, particularly at this point in the life of the person with the illness. There is little to lose and much to gain from speaking openly and listening earnestly to one another.

Interpersonal Mindfulness

Interpersonal mindfulness involves being authentic, speaking truthfully, and listening sincerely. If you're like many, you may recall occasions when you spoke too soon and then felt frustrated that the message was not adequately conveyed. Or you searched for the right words to say, yet they didn't seem to come. Or you rehearsed over and over in your mind what you were going to say, only to find that the conversation ended up stilted and lacked sufficient depth.

The well-established four-step process called *insight dialogue*, originated by Greg Kramer, is a form of interpersonal mindfulness that facilitates thoughtful and meaningful exchanges (Kramer 2007). Insight dialogue is particularly well suited for the difficult conversations just described. This kind of communication is not forced, rushed, or rehearsed. It's best to begin by just sitting quietly and being present with the other person for a few minutes. The four steps are:

1. *Pause.* Before you speak, stop. Simply dwell in your internal present-moment experience for a few moments, noticing your bodily sensations, your thoughts, and your emotional feelings.

2. *Relax.* Allow your mind and body to calm. Bring awareness to the rhythm of your breath or another neutral focus. You may also bring awareness to parts of your body that feel tense. Breathe into those areas and notice the tension dissolve.

3. *Open.* Be open to the fullness of your current experience outside of your body, sensing the other person near you and the qualities of the setting (like color, light, air movement, and temperature).

4. *Trust emergence.* Let go of preconceptions and trust the unfolding experience

5. *Listen deeply.* With attentiveness and receptivity, surrender fully to the words and presence of the other person and listen to your inner voice.

6. *Speak the truth.* Allow your words to flow spontaneously, speaking honestly and with kindness.

～ REFLECTIVE PRACTICE ～
Preparing for Difficult Conversations

This practice can consist of reflection only or may also involve writing, whichever you prefer.

- Settle your mind and body by noticing your breathing or some other neutral point of awareness. Rest in this awareness for a few moments.

- Ask yourself: *Have I said all that I want to say to the significant people in my life? Is there someone (or more than one person) whom I need to talk to but have held back from?*

- If you realize that you feel the need to speak with someone yet haven't done so, ask yourself:

  Whom do I need to speak with?

117

What do I want to tell this person?
What is holding me back?
What do I (or we) lose by being reticent?
What do I (or we) gain from speaking up?
How can I facilitate this conversation?

- Close your eyes for a moment and notice how you feel right now.

Each Day...

Pause before speaking. Then speak honestly and wholeheartedly. Listen attentively in a way that genuinely conveys kindness and interest.

Keep in Mind

Holding back from talking about difficult topics creates tension within you and between you and others. Also, you may lose the opportunity to say what you need to say if you continue to wait for the right moment. Communication grounded in truthfulness, caring, and respect can promote inner healing and mutual understanding.

If you are struggling with broaching the difficult subject or if you feel that your family members may react very negatively or impulsively, you may want to initiate communication with a sincere note or letter that summarizes your feelings or wishes, rather than start off with a face-to-face conversation. This could give your loved ones an opportunity to reflect on your words, which can then set the stage for a candid and essential dialogue.

11

~

WITHOUT WORDS:
THE POWER OF
PRESENCE AND TOUCH

Silence
is an ocean. Speech is a river.
When the ocean is searching for you, don't walk
to the language-river. Listen to the ocean,
and bring your talky business
to an end.

—Rumi, *The Essential Rumi*

While verbal communication is potent, communicating without words is equally so. The power of presence and touch cannot be underestimated. There are times when words are simply inadequate or superfluous, and there are times when speaking is just too much effort or impossible.

Robert, a seventy-two-year-old retired lawyer, had a progressive neuro-muscular disorder that affected many of his functional abilities, including walking, talking, writing, and eating. He was mentally sharp, yet he tired easily and was spending an increasing amount of time in bed, listening to audiobooks, Mozart, and guided meditations. He had had a close relationship with his family over the years, and they had been very supportive throughout his illness. However, over time they became less involved in his care because of the additional help of round-the-clock home health aides. His wife, Abigail, and his two grown children, Jessica and John, felt frustrated, because they sensed a growing separation from Robert due to his inability to interact with them. Robert, too, was frustrated and felt isolated. He was saddened by the palpable distance from his loved ones and yearned to feel reconnected with his wife, daughter, and son.

Robert and his family believed that they couldn't communicate with one another. They simply failed to realize that there are enormous opportunities to communicate without words, through presence and touch.

Presence is a state of being receptive and attentive to another in the midst of a caring and spacious silence. *Touch*, as used in this book, means the tactile connection from one person to another through skin-to-skin contact. Simply being present with one another, with or without touch, often is enough to convey love and compassion, and to maintain, and perhaps deepen, a mutual experience of connectedness. The truth is that our presence and touch are the greatest gifts of self that we can give to one another.

Presence

Sometimes words can get in the way of truly bonding with others. Language can clutter in a manner that distracts and consequently keeps interactions at a superficial level. There are many occasions when simply *being with* another is enough. There is fullness, richness, and intimacy to the shared experience of sitting quietly beside one another that transcends verbal communication, like sitting together quietly viewing the sunset. What is conveyed is beyond words. In her book *Being with Dying: Cultivating Compassion and Fearlessness in the Presence of Death*, Roshi Joan Halifax extensively explores the essential role that presence has at the end of life for the person who is dying, the person's loved ones, and the professional caregivers involved. She writes (Halifax 2009, 10): "Often we feel that silence and still-ness aren't good enough when suffering is present. We feel compelled to 'do something': to talk, console, work, clean, move around, 'help.' But in the shared embrace of meditation, a caregiver and dying person can be held in an intimate silence beyond consolation or assistance... Does anything really need to be said? Can I know greater intimacy with her through a mutuality beyond words and actions? Can I relax and trust in simply being there, with-out needing my personality to mediate the tender connection we share?"

Silence

Silence is generally not valued in our society and indeed is rarely put into practice in everyday life. Very commonly, pauses during conversations are quickly filled with words due to conditioning and also a person's discom-fort or desire to keep emotional distance.

You may recognize that there are times when being in silence with another person is more comfortable than at other times. Consider instances when it has been relatively easy for you to be in silence and other instances when it was challenging. What do you think distinguishes the two?

In a paper that I cowrote with colleagues Tony Back, Roshi Joan Halifax, and Cynda Rushton, we identified and discussed different types of silence (Back et al. 2009). While some silences can feel awkward, indifferent, hos-tile, or forced, there are other silences that feel comforting, affirming, and safe. We have termed this latter type of silence *compassionate silence*. Compassionate silence has a moment-by-moment quality and a profound sense of being with and standing with another that can nurture a mutual sense of understanding and caring. Even though our paper was written for doctors and nurses, the concept of compassionate silence applies to every-one. You and your loved ones can explore how to bring compassionate silences into your daily lives to foster presence and connectedness.

~ REFLECTIVE PRACTICE ~
Opening to Presence

Do this practice with another person, someone with whom you share a positive connection and who is receptive to doing it with you.

- Sit or lie beside one another in silence. Do not speak during this practice.

- Do not touch one another; simply *be* next to each other.

- Softly gaze in front of you (neutral point of focus) or close your eyes. Do not look into each other's eyes.

- Notice how you feel: bodily sensations, emotions, and your overall body.

- Bring awareness to the natural rhythm of your breathing for a minute or two.

- Turn toward one another, and if your eyes have been closed, open them to a soft gaze. Expand your awareness to your loved one's breathing, noticing the movement of the person's chest or abdomen with each inbreath and outbreath.

- Simultaneously bring awareness to your breathing *and* your loved one's breathing. For a few minutes, rest in awareness of each other's breathing. Notice if your breathing naturally becomes synchronized. Simply notice and do not try to change your breathing in any way.

- Notice how you feel: bodily sensations, emotional feeling tones, and your overall body.

- Now softly gaze into one another's eyes.

- While gently looking at each other, be aware of your breathing, your loved one's breathing, and the sense of being next to each other. Rest in this awareness for a minute or two.

- Notice how you feel: bodily sensations, emotional feeling tones, and your overall body. Consider how you felt when you started and how you feel now.

Touch

The power of touch, physical contact with another, cannot be underestimated. We know that premature babies thrive when they are touched and held. Similarly, adults do as well. Touch promotes relaxation, reduces stress, increases our sense of well-being, and unites us with others, physically and energetically, in harmonious ways that words and merely being with others do not. Some people have an aversion to touch and describe themselves as "not touchy-feely." Even with such people, very simple touch, as little as fingertip to fingertip or holding hands, likely won't overwhelm the person, and it can promote a healing connection between you and another person.

Being Touched

Family members and other loved ones often feel powerless when they don't know what they could do to make you feel better. They may want to connect with you, without knowing how best to convey their love for you. Touch offers an opportunity for both: a way for your loved ones to feel that they are helping and making you feel better *and* a way for them to nonverbally express love and care for you.

Social worker and researcher William Collinge and colleagues have developed a program available on DVD that teaches family members very simple touch and massage techniques to use on loved ones with cancer (Collinge 2008; Collinge et al. 2011; Collinge et al. 2007). The DVD demonstrates safe and easy techniques, such as gently massaging hands, feet, or scalp (Collinge 2009). For people with illness, their symptoms, such as pain and anxiety, are alleviated by their loved ones' touch. They also describe how their relationships have been strengthened as a result. Additionally, family members feel empowered by using touch as a means of enhancing the life of a partner or spouse, parent, sibling, or child who is sick.

Therapeutic massage provided by licensed massage therapists can be tremendously beneficial by promoting mental and physical relaxation and alleviating pain. Research in this area has demonstrated the positive effects of therapeutic massage on the quality of life in people with serious illness, particularly when used in combination with meditation (Downey et al. 2009; Williams et al. 2005).

Touching Others

Touch can be reciprocal. Rather than just being touched by others, you may also consider how you can reach out and physically touch others. This can include extending your hand to initiate contact and hold hands, or gently stroking or rubbing lotion on your loved ones' hands or feet, if you are able. It need not take much of your energy. You, too, may feel helpless because you are not able to care for others in the manner that you used to. So giving to others through your touch and simple massage can make you feel helpful and make others feel good.

Reaching out and touching others goes beyond people. Touching pets can be deeply comforting, even more so than touching humans. Dogs and cats have a warm and unconditional presence, which invites us to express our love and connect with them through our hands.

~ REFLECTIVE PRACTICE ~
Touching and Being Touched

Either through reflection alone or through reflection and writing, consider your relationship with touch.

- What are the different ways you are touched?

  What does it feel like to be touched?

Are you comfortable being touched? Do you like being touched?

Are there certain people whom you prefer to be touched by? Do they know that you like to be touched?

- What are the different ways that you physically touch others?

What does it feel like to initiate touch?

Are you comfortable initiating touch?

Are there certain people whom you prefer to touch? Do they know that you like to touch them?

- Consider the ways in which you can expand the practice of touch in your life, either through being touched or reaching out and touching someone.

Each Day...

For a few minutes, sit in silence with and gently touch someone you care about. If you are comfortable doing so, invite someone you love to massage you hands, feet, or neck.

Keep in Mind

Communicating without words is powerful. Silent and compassionate presence is receptive and spacious. Simple touch, like holding hands or gently stroking or massaging easily accessible areas, is mutually comforting. Presence and touch can foster healing and connectedness between you and your loved ones in ways that transcend words.

12

~

THRIVING TODAY

He who has a why to live can bear almost any how.
—Friedrich Nietzsche

Renowned psychiatrist and Holocaust survivor Viktor Frankl shares his observations from his time in the concentration camps during World War II, noting, "Life holds a potential meaning under any conditions, even the most miserable ones" (Frankl 1984). His inspiring words point to the possibility for you, too, to find meaning in your life despite physical and mental challenges.

You may find that incessant worries and fears cloud your ability to see what gives your life meaning. You may have lost touch with what nourishes and energizes your spirit, or circumstances may have changed in such a way that what used to bring meaning to your life may no longer be accessible to you. You may have become bitter toward your current circumstances or disenchanted by actual or perceived limitations to having a meaningful life.

Cultivating mindfulness, as described extensively in part 1 of this book, can open you to see more clearly and take inventory of what matters most to you. It can also help you to assess realistically what you're capable of doing and how to meaningfully prioritize the precious time that you have remaining. The cultivation of compassion and related interpersonal qualities—like kindness, forgiveness, generosity, empathetic joy, and gratitude—as explored in part 2 of this book, can foster your heart to open and heal. Mindfulness plus compassion meld to create a rich sense of connectedness—connecting you with your inner wisdom, your significant relationships, others near and far who may be suffering, the natural world, and, for some, a higher being, like God. Collectively, mindfulness, compassion, and connectedness can help you to remember, or *re-member* (to be a part of a whole again), what matters most to you.

To thrive means to expand, flourish, and grow vigorously. This term is used to describe plants, babies, and the human spirit. It is this latter depiction that relates to you. You may question if and how it's possible for you to expand and grow at this point in your life. You may not be able to do what you used to do physically, like exercising or working, or even mentally, like remembering facts or doing computations. Yet, you can still curiously approach each day and gain new insights about yourself and the world around you, and you can still leave fingerprints on people and things you touch. Tapping into what gives your life meaning can enable you to flourish and also leave an indelible legacy. Other ways you can thrive include being flexible and willing to try new things; doing fulfilling and enjoyable activities; having supportive and trusted relationships; expressing yourself authentically; partnering with your health care team; having a spiritual connection, including with nature; and infusing your day with fun and laughter.

Thriving today means living fully at this moment in time—recognizing what matters most and experiencing vividness and satisfaction in life's simplicities, as well as kindheartedness and joy with others. In doing so, you can maximize the quality of your life and the quality of your relationships today and leave a positive and enduring impact for the future.

～ REFLECTIVE PRACTICE ～
What Matters Most and Setting Priorities

You can do this practice through quiet reflection only or with the addition of writing in a journal.

- Pause briefly, even for just a moment or two; ground yourself in the present-moment experience; be aware of the sensations in your body; or listen and look around you.

- Reflect on what is most important to you at this phase of your life.

  People or pets you care about the most

  Wishes that remain unfulfilled

  Legacies you want to leave behind

  Spiritual connections you'd like to develop or strengthen

- Consider if you are spending enough of your time connecting with what matters most to you.

- Reflect on what you can do to be authentic with yourself and live with meaning.

- Among the different things that matter to you, choose your top three priorities.

- Identify specific areas of these three priorities that you would like to expand and develop.

Final Reflections

This book has accompanied you through a journey of self-exploration. It has changed nothing except that it has helped you wake up to your own inner wisdom, open your heart, and reconnect with others and the world around you. The practices in this book are not play rehearsals or music lessons to be performed at certain times on certain days. They are living practices that can become a part of your daily approach to life.

Living with a serious illness and facing your mortality need not be fraught with dread and despair. The fundamental good nature of who you are doesn't falter, regardless of what is happening internally and externally. It sometimes might be hidden by mental agitation, distractions, or discomfort, just as dark clouds might temporarily obscure the unremitting light and warmth of the sun, but it is always there. Mindfulness, compassion, and connectedness, qualities you can cultivate through practices described throughout this book, foster a sense of *being with* and *opening to*, rather than resisting or retreating. They help your true essence to shine brightly, which will be your beacon to see what matters most, to feel whole and live fully, to sustain you through occasional storms, and, ultimately, to die more peacefully. Therefore, it is essential that you take the time and attention to tend to your own needs. My hope is that you will keep these chapters and stories that I have shared with you in your heart and your mind. Beyond just getting by and merely surviving, living fully and thriving today is possible. Are you ready?

Starting here, what do you want to remember?
How sunlight creeps along a shining floor?
What scent of old wood hovers, what softened
sound from outside fills the air?

Will you ever bring a better gift for the world
than the breathing respect that you carry
wherever you go right now? Are you waiting
for time to show you some better thoughts?

When you turn around, starting here, lift this
new glimpse that you found; carry into evening
all that you want from this day. This interval you spent
reading or hearing this, keep it for life—

What can anyone give you greater than now,
starting here, right in this room, when you turn around?

—William Stafford, "You Reading This, Be Ready,"
from *The Way It Is: New and Selected Poems*

RESOURCES

Guided mindfulness and compassion meditation audio recordings based on the practices described in this book are available as CDs or downloadable MP3 files. The author, Susan Bauer-Wu, also facilitates workshops and retreats for people with life-limiting illness and their families, as well as trainings and retreats for health care professionals. You can find information on how to order the guided meditations and a listing of workshops and retreats at the Thriving Today website: thrivingtoday.com.

The Upaya Institute sponsors a number of contemplative-practice training programs and meditation retreats, including the professional training program, Being with Dying, held at the Upaya Zen Center in Santa Fe, New Mexico. You can find a listing and descriptions of the programs at www .upaya.org.

The University of Massachusetts Medical School Center for Mindfulness in Medicine, Health Care, and Society sponsors a variety of mindfulness-based training programs and an annual conference. You can find information about the programs and also guided meditation recordings by Center for Mindfulness instructors at umassmed.edu/cfm/home/index.aspx. You can order meditation practice CDs by Jon Kabat-Zinn at www.mindfulness tapes.com.

The inspiring and effective DVD program, *Touch, Caring, and Cancer*, provides simple instruction for family and friends to use safe, simple touch techniques to comfort their loved ones with cancer (it can also be used with anyone with a serious illness). You can find information on this DVD, an illustrated manual, and online support at partnersinhealing.net.

The Center for Communication in Medicine has produced thoughtful films for patients, families, and health care professionals. The center's DVDs and workbooks facilitate communication among patients, families, and health care professionals about the meaning of "incurable but treatable" diagnoses, treatment choices, quality-of-life issues, and preferences for end-of-life care. For more information, visit communicationinmedicine.org.

REFERENCES

Austin, James H. 2009. *Selfless Insight: Zen and the Meditative Transformations of Consciousness.* Cambridge, MA: MIT Press.

Back, Anthony L., Susan M. Bauer-Wu, Cynda H. Rushton, and Joan Halifax. 2009. "Compassionate Silence in the Patient–Clinician Encounter: A Contemplative Approach." *Journal of Palliative Medicine* 12 (12):1113–17.

Bauer-Wu, Susan, Amy M. Sullivan, Elana Rosenbaum, Mary Jane Ott, Mark Powell, Margo McLoughlin, and Martha W. Healey. 2008. "Facing the Challenges of Hematopoietic Stem Cell Transplantation with Mindfulness Meditation: A Pilot Study." *Integrative Cancer Therapies* 7 (2):62–69.

Beech/Rangoon, Hannah. 2010. "Aung San Suu Kyi: Burma's First Lady of Freedom." *Time,* December 29, www.time.com/time/world/article/0,8599,2039939-1,00.html.

Bohlmeijer, Ernst, Rilana Prenger, Erik Taal, and Pim Cuijpers. 2010. "The Effects of Mindfulness-Based Stress Reduction Therapy on Mental Health of Adults with a Chronic Medical Disease: A Meta-Analysis." *Journal of Psychosomatic Research* 68 (6):539–44.

Bohlmeijer, Ernst, Filip Smit, and Pim Cuijpers. 2003. "Effects of Reminiscence and Life Review on Late-Life Depression: A Meta-Analysis." *International Journal of Geriatric Psychiatry* 18 (12):1088–94.

Boyce, Barry. 2011. "The Power of Mindfulness: Jon Kabat-Zinn, Daniel Siegel, and Susan Bauer-Wu on Why Mindfulness Heals and How to Do It." *Shambhala Sun*, January, 42–50.

Brefczynski-Lewis, Julie A., Andre Lutz, Hillary S. Schaefer, D. B. Levinson, and Richard J. Davidson. 2007. "Neural Correlates of Attentional Expertise in Long-Term Meditation Practitioners." *Proceedings of the National Academy of Sciences* 104 (27):11483–88.

Carlson, Linda E., Michael Speca, Peter Faris, and Kamala D. Patel. 2007. "One Year Pre-Post Intervention Follow-Up of Psychological, Immune, Endocrine, and Blood Pressure Outcomes of Mindfulness-Based Stress Reduction (MBSR) in Breast and Prostate Cancer Outpatients." *Brain, Behavior, and Immunity* 21 (8):1038–49.

Carmody, James, and Ruth Baer. 2008. "Relationships between Mindfulness Practice and Levels of Mindfulness, Medical and Psychological Symptoms, and Well-Being in a Mindfulness-Based Stress Reduction Program." *Journal of Behavioral Medicine* 31 (1):23–33.

Carson, James W., Francis J. Keefe, Thomas R. Lynch, Kimberly M. Carson, Veeraindar Goli, Anne Marie Fras, and Steven R. Thorp. 2005. "Loving-Kindness Meditation for Chronic Low Back Pain: Results from a Pilot Trial." *Journal of Holistic Nursing* 23 (3):287–304.

Chiesa, Alberto, and Alessandro Serretti. 2010. "A Systematic Review of Neurobiological and Clinical Features of Mindfulness Meditations." *Psychological Medicine* 40 (8):1239–52.

Collinge, William. 2008. *Partners in Healing: Simple Ways to Offer Support, Comfort, and Care to a Loved One Facing Illness*. Boston: Trumpeter Books.

————. 2009. *Touch, Caring, and Cancer: Simple Instruction for Family and Friends*. DVD and manual. Kittery Point, ME: Collinge and Associates.

Collinge, William, Janet Kahn, Tracy Walton, Susan Bauer-Wu, Leila Kozak, Mary Malinski, Kenneth Fletcher, Paul Yarnold, and Robert Soltysik. 2011. "Cancer Patient Symptom Reduction: A Randomized Controlled

Trial of Family Caregiver Multimedia Instruction in Touch and Massage." Unpublished working copy.

Collinge, William, Janet Kahn, Paul Yarnold, Susan Bauer-Wu, and Ruth McCorkle. 2007. "Couples and Cancer: Feasibility of Brief Instruction in Massage and Touch Therapy to Build Caregiver Efficacy." *Journal of the Society of Integrative Oncology* 5 (4):147–54.

Creswell, J. David, Hector F. Myers, Steven W. Cole, and Michael R. Irwin. 2009. "Mindfulness Meditation Training Effects on CD4+ T Lymphocytes in HIV-1 Infected Adults: A Small Randomized Controlled Trial." *Brain, Behavior, and Immunity* 23 (2):184–88.

Creswell, J. David, Baldwin M. Way, Naomi I. Eisenberger, and Matthew D. Lieberman. 2007. "Neural Correlates of Dispositional Mindfulness during Affect Labeling." *Psychosomatic Medicine* 69 (6):560–65.

Dalen, Jeanne, Bruce W. Smith, Brian M. Shelley, Anita Lee Sloan, Lisa Leahigh, and Debbie Begay. 2010. "Pilot Study: Mindful Eating and Living (MEAL): Weight, Eating Behavior, and Psychological Outcomes Associated with a Mindfulness-Based Intervention for People with Obesity." *Complementary Therapies in Medicine* 18 (6):260–64.

Davidson, Richard J., Jon Kabat-Zinn, Jessica Schumacher, Melissa Rosenkranz, Daniel Muller, Saki F. Santorelli, Ferris Urbanowski, Anne Harrington, Katherine Bonus, and John F. Sheridan. 2003. "Alterations in Brain and Immune Function Produced by Mindfulness Meditation." *Psychosomatic Medicine* 65 (4):564–70.

Downey, Lois, Ruth A. Engelberg, Leanna J. Standish, Leila Kozak, and William E. Lafferty. 2009. "Three Lessons from a Randomized Trial of Massage and Meditation at End of Life: Patient Benefit, Outcome Measure Selection, and Design of Trials with Terminally Ill Patients." *American Journal of Hospice and Palliative Care* 26 (4):246–53.

Emmons, Robert A., and Michael E. McCullough. 2003. "Counting Blessings versus Burdens: An Experimental Investigation of Gratitude and

Subjective Well-Being in Daily Life." *Journal of Personality and Social Psychology* 84 (2):377–89.

Farb, Norman A. S., Zindel V. Segal, Helen Mayberg, Jim Bean, Deborah McKeon, Zainab Fatima, and Adam K. Anderson. 2007. "Attending to the Present: Mindfulness Meditation Reveals Distinct Neural Modes of Self-Reference." *Social Cognitive and Affective Neuroscience* 2 (4):313–22.

Frankl, Viktor E. 1984. *Man's Search for Meaning.* New York: Simon & Schuster.

Fredrickson, Barbara L. 2001. "The Role of Positive Emotions in Positive Psychology: The Broaden-and-Build Theory of Positive Emotions." *American Psychologist* 56 (3):218–26.

Fredrickson, Barbara L., Michael A. Cohn, Kimberly A. Coffey, Jolynn Pek, and Sandra M. Finkel. 2008. "Open Hearts Build Lives: Positive Emotions, Induced through Loving-Kindness Meditation, Build Consequential Personal Resources." *Journal of Personality and Social Psychology* 95 (5):1045–62.

Goldin, Phillippe, Wiveka Ramel, and James Gross. 2009. "Mindfulness Meditation Training and Self-Referential Processing in Social Anxiety Disorder: Behavioral and Neural Effects." *Journal of Cognitive Psychotherapy* 23:242–57.

Grossman, Paul, Ludwig Kappos, H. Gensicke, Manoranjan D'Souza, David C. Mohr, Iris K. Penner, and C. Steiner. 2010. "MS Quality of Life, Depression, and Fatigue Improve after Mindfulness Training: A Randomized Trial." *Neurology* 75 (13):1141–49.

Grossman, Paul, Ludger Niemann, Stefan Schmidt, and Harald Walach. 2004. "Mindfulness-Based Stress Reduction and Health Benefits: A Meta-Analysis." *Journal of Psychosomatic Research* 57 (1):35–43.

Halifax, Joan. 2009. *Being with Dying: Cultivating Compassion and Fearlessness in the Presence of Death.* Boston: Shambhala Publications.

Hanser, Suzanne B., Susan Bauer-Wu, Lorrie Kubicek, Martha Healey, Judith Manola, Maria Hernandez, and Craig Bunnell. 2006. "Effects of a

Music Therapy Intervention on Quality of Life and Distress in Women with Metastatic Breast Cancer." *Journal of the Society for Integrative Oncology* 4 (3):116–24.

Hutcherson, Cendri A., Emma M. Seppala, and James J. Gross. 2008. "Loving-Kindness Meditation Increases Social Connectedness." *Emotion* 8 (5):720–24.

Jain, Shamini, Shauna L. Shapiro, Summer Swanick, Scott C. Roesch, Paul J. Mills, Iris Bell, and Gary E. Schwartz. 2007. "A Randomized Controlled Trial of Mindfulness Meditation versus Relaxation Training: Effects on Distress, Positive States of Mind, Rumination, and Distraction." *Annals of Behavioral Medicine* 33 (1):11–21.

Jam, Sara, Amir Hossein Imani, Maryam Foroughi, SeyedAhmad SeyedAlinaghi, Hamid Emadi Koochak, and Minoo Mohraz. 2010. "The Effects of Mindfulness-Based Stress Reduction (MBSR) Program in Iranian HIV/AIDS Patients: A Pilot Study." *Acta Medica Iranica* 48 (2):101–6.

Jha, Amishi P., Jason Krompinger, and Michael J. Baime. 2007. "Mindfulness Training Modifies Subsystems of Attention." *Cognitive, Affective, and Behavioral Neuroscience* 7 (2):109–19.

Kabat-Zinn, Jon. 1990. *Full Catastrophe Living: Using the Wisdom of Your Body and Mind to Face Stress, Pain, and Illness.* New York: Delta.

Kim, Borah, Sang-Hyuk Lee, Yong Woo Kim, Tai Kiu Choi, Keunyoung Yook, Shin Young Suh, Sung Joon Cho, and Ki-Hwan Yook. 2010. "Effectiveness of a Mindfulness-Based Cognitive Therapy Program as an Adjunct to Pharmacotherapy in Patients with Panic Disorder." *Journal of Anxiety Disorders* 24 (6):590–95.

Kramer, Gregory. 2007. *Insight Dialogue: The Interpersonal Path to Freedom.* Boston: Shambhala Publications.

Kreitzer, Mary Jo, Cynthia R. Gross, Xiaoyun Ye, Valerie Russas, and Charoen Treesak. 2005. "Longitudinal Impact of Mindfulness Meditation on Illness Burden in Solid-Organ Transplant Recipients." *Progress in Transplantation* 15 (2):166–72.

Lazar, Sara W., Catherine E. Kerr, Rachel H. Wasserman, Jeremy R. Gray, Douglas N. Greve, Michael T. Treadway, et al. 2005. "Meditation Experience Is Associated with Increased Cortical Thickness." *NeuroReport* 16 (17):1893–97.

Leary, Mark R., Eleanor B. Tate, Claire E. Adams, Ashley Batts Allen, and Jessica Hancock. 2007. "Self-Compassion and Reactions to Unpleasant Self-Relevant Events: The Implications of Treating Oneself Kindly." *Journal of Personality and Social Psychology* 92 (5):887–904.

Ledesma, Dianne, and Hiroaki Kumano. 2009. "Mindfulness-Based Stress Reduction and Cancer: A Meta-Analysis." *Psycho-Oncology* 18 (6):571–79.

Lutz, Antoine, Julie Brefczynski-Lewis, Tom Johnstone, and Richard J. Davidson. 2008. "Regulation of the Neural Circuitry of Emotion by Compassion Meditation: Effects of Meditative Expertise." *PLoS ONE* 3 (3):e1897. doi:10.1371/journal.pone.0001897.

Lutz, Antoine, Lawrence L. Greischar, Nancy B. Rawlings, Matthieu Ricard, and Richard J. Davidson. 2004. "Long-Term Meditators Self-Induce High-Amplitude Gamma Synchrony during Mental Practice." *Proceedings of the National Academy of Sciences* 101 (46):16369–73.

Lutz, Antoine, Heleen A. Slagter, John D. Dunne, and Richard J. Davidson. 2008. "Attention Regulation and Monitoring in Meditation." *Trends in Cognitive Sciences* 12 (4):163–69.

McCullough, Michael E., Robert A. Emmons, and Jo-Ann Tsang. 2002. "The Grateful Disposition: A Conceptual and Empirical Topography." *Journal of Personality and Social Psychology* 82 (1):112–27.

Messias, Erick, Anil Saini, Philip Sinato, and Stephen Welch. 2010. "Bearing Grudges and Physical Health: Relationship to Smoking, Cardiovascular Health, and Ulcers." *Social Psychiatry and Psychiatric Epidemiology* 45 (2):183–87.

Moore, Adam, and Peter Malinowski. 2009. "Meditation, Mindfulness, and Cognitive Flexibility." *Consciousness and Cognition* 18 (1):176–86.

Pace, Thaddeus W. W., Lobsang Tenzin Negi, Daniel D. Adame, Steven P. Cole, Teresa I. Sivilli, Timothy D. Brown, Michael J. Issa, and Charles L. Raison. 2009. "Effect of Compassion Meditation on Neuroendocrine, Innate Immune, and Behavioral Responses to Psychosocial Stress." *Psychoneuroendocrinology* 34 (1):87–98.

Prochaska, James O., and Wayne F. Velicer. 1997. "The Transtheoretical Model of Health Behavior Change." *American Journal Health Promotion* 12 (1):38–48.

Ricard, Matthieu. 2010. *Why Meditate? Working with Thoughts and Emotions.* Translated by Sherab Chodzin Kohn. Carlsbad, CA: Hay House, Inc.

Salzberg, Sharon. 2004. *Lovingkindness: The Revolutionary Art of Happiness.* Boston: Shambhala Publications.

Schwartz, Carolyn, Janice Bell Meisenhelder, Yunsheng Ma, and George Reed. 2003. "Altruistic Social Interest Behaviors Are Associated with Better Mental Health." *Psychosomatic Medicine* 65 (5):778–85.

Singer, Tania, Ben Seymour, John O'Doherty, Holger Kaube, Raymond J. Dolan, and Chris D. Frith. 2004. "Empathy for Pain Involves the Affective but Not Sensory Components of Pain." *Science* 303 (5661):1157–62.

Slagter, Heleen A., Antoine Lutz, Lawrence L. Greischar, Andrew D. Francis, Sander Nieuwenhuis, James M. Davis, and Richard J. Davidson. 2007. "Mental Training Affects Distribution of Limited Brain Resources." *PLoS Biology* 5 (6):e138. doi:10.1371/journal.pbio.0050138.

Steindl-Rast, David. 1984. *Gratefulness, the Heart of Prayer: An Approach to Life in Fullness.* Ramsey, NJ: Paulist Press.

Sullivan, Martin J., Laura Wood, Jennifer Terry, Jeff Brantley, Ann Charles, Vicky McGee, et al. 2009. "The Support, Education, and Research in Chronic Heart Failure Study (SEARCH): A Mindfulness-Based Psychoeducational Intervention Improves Depression and Clinical

Symptoms in Patients with Chronic Heart Failure." *American Heart Journal* 157 (1):84–90.

Teasdale, John D., Richard G. Moore, Hazel Hayhurst, Marie Pope, Susan Williams, and Zindel V. Segal. 2002. "Metacognitive Awareness and Prevention of Relapse in Depression: Empirical Evidence." *Journal of Consulting and Clinical Psychology* 70 (2):275–87.

Temel, Jennifer S., Joseph A. Greer, Alona Muzikansky, Emily R. Gallagher, Sonal Admane, Vicki A. Jackson, et al. 2010. "Early Palliative Care for Patients with Metastatic Non–Small-Cell Lung Cancer." *New England Journal of Medicine* 363 (8):733–42.

vanOyen Witvliet, Charlotte, Thomas E. Ludwig, and Kelly L. Vander Laan. 2001. "Granting Forgiveness or Harboring Grudges: Implications for Emotion, Physiology, and Health." *Psychological Science* 12 (2):117–23.

Williams, Anna-Leila, Peter A. Selwyn, Lauren Liberti, Susan Molde, Valentine Yanchou Njike, Ruth McCorkle, Daniel Zelterman, and David L. Katz. 2005. "A Randomized Controlled Trial of Meditation and Massage Effects on Quality of Life in People with Late-Stage Disease: A Pilot Study." *Journal of Palliative Medicine* 8 (5):939–52.

Witek-Janusek, Linda, Kevin Albuquerque, Karen Rambo Chroniak, Christopher Chroniak, Ramon Durazo-Arvizu, and Herbert L. Mathews. 2008. "Effect of Mindfulness Based Stress Reduction on Immune Function, Quality of Life, and Coping in Women Newly Diagnosed with Early Stage Breast Cancer." *Brain, Behavior, and Immunity* 22 (6):969–81.

Witkiewitz, Katie, and Sarah Bowen. 2010. "Depression, Craving, and Substance Use Following a Randomized Trial of Mindfulness-Based Relapse Prevention." *Journal of Consulting and Clinical Psychology* 78 (3):362–74.

Worthington Jr., Everett L., Charlotte vanOyen Witvliet, Andrea J. Lerner, and Michael Scherer. 2005. "Forgiveness in Health Research and Medical Practice." *Explore* 1 (3):169–76.

Susan Bauer-Wu, PhD, RN, integrates her scientific research in mind-body medicine, clinical experience as an oncology, psychiatric, and hospice nurse, and personal meditation practice to improve the well-being of those living with serious illness and their loved ones. She is currently associate professor of nursing at Emory University in Atlanta, GA, and was previously an instructor of medicine at Harvard Medical School in Boston, MA. She lives in Atlanta, GA, and Brookline, MA.

Bauer-Wu has had a productive program of research focused on the effects of chronic stress and the benefits of mindfulness and compassion practices in the face of debilitating and potentially life-limiting illness. She has provided significant service and leadership to major national and international organizations and has earned several esteemed awards. In addition, she teaches training programs on mindfulness-based stress reduction and contemplative end-of-life care, and also facilitates resiliency retreats and workshops for health care professionals as well as patients and families affected by chronic medical conditions.

Foreword writer **Joan Halifax, PhD**, is a medical anthropologist, Buddhist teacher, and author of *Being with Dying* and other books. She is founder, abbot, and head teacher at Upaya Zen Center, a Buddhist monastery in Santa Fe, NM, and director of the Upaya Institute. She has served as visiting faculty and lectured on the subject of death and dying at many academic institutions throughout the United States and abroad.

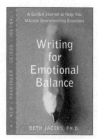